WHAT THEY'RE SAYING ABOUT THIS BOOK

"My husband, Jack, says this is a very meaningful book.... As he reads it, he is wiping his eyes a lot and I consider that the best sign of a best seller."

Dee Slocum, Author of: Daisy, A wild duck's story and Welcome Aboard Jack's or Better.

"Well written. I found it very enjoyable reading. Humorous, yet at times it had me nearly in tears. I particularly enjoyed the three patriotic poems in the LIFE'S LESSONS chapter."

Stephen D. Clifton, US Army, Sergeant Major, Retired.

"..... debut into the world of publication took me on a rollercoaster ride of heartbreak, humor, and happiness. I found it very intriguing and engaging... ....difficult to put it down. You'll want to finish the entire book in one sitting."

D. Chandler,   contributor @ TCPalm.com

"I loved the book. It is captivating and reads like a novel even though it is in rhyme...... I feel others would find help, comfort and/or encouragement from reading it, just as I did;"

Judy Craddock, lifelong best friend of Christine, one of the primary characters and the author's deceased wife, who was taken by cancer at the tender young age of 40.

A PURSUIT OF LIFE

ISBN: 978-0-9826168-4-0

Cover Design: Walter Bodie

Published by Fiction Publishing, Inc.
5626 Travelers Way
Fort Pierce, FL 34982

First Edition

A PURSUIT OF LIFE

A BOOK OF POEMS

FROM THE MIND OF A WIDOWER

BY:

RICHARD LEE KING
Dickking44@yahoo.com

PRELUDE

This book is a poetic telling of a love that didn't die with death and that living couldn't extinguish until time brought it full circle. As the author puts it, "This book is *kinda, sorta* my life story." Commencing just moments after his birth, he takes you on an imaginary journey through his childhood, his subsequent 20 year marriage to Christine, her death, then through his struggles to overcome despair and finally to the pinnacle of new love. You are there from the very beginning, where he states: *"After nine months of darkness in a tiny 98 degree room, suddenly it's 68 and very bright, as I come out of the womb. I've nothing but the air I breathe and not a stitch of clothing. They spank me on the butt and that really starts me loathing."*

It was just after the great depression and "We didn't *'live too high on the hog,'* however we were not alone. Everyone *'was in the same boat'* and to be quite honest about it, I don't remember thinking we were any worse off than anyone else. We knew no difference"

As you travel through his childhood, growing up in rural, post depression Michigan, he writes *"We hunted and trapped and fished through the ice. We squabbled and fought, then tried to make nice."* Later he marries his high school sweetheart and the two of them raise two baby boys into strapping young men, whereupon she becomes fatally afflicted with breast cancer. He writes of her impending death; *"We weren't really religious, but we learned to pray, hoping that a miracle just might come our way. With all of my being I tried hard to believe that, for someone this special, He'd grant a reprieve. Church every Sunday, faith healers and all, hoping that somehow, He'd answer our call. Then as I stood there overlooking her casket, I had a question for Him, but I never did ask it."*

After much soul searching and guilt trips down several wrong roads he finally falls in love with the lady he considers as the equal of that first love from nearly fifty years earlier. And he writes; *"Their paths crossed, like a head on collision. She could be no more perfect, had she come in a vision. Had he dreamed her up, to be precise, he wouldn't have dreamed her to be this nice."*

You are there as he is *"Nearing the End,"* where he leads off a poem with: *"Well, I've been down that road and I've been up the creek. I'm not over the hill, but I'm getting close to the peak. If you get what you pay for and you pay for what you get, oh Lord, I've been wondering ain't I done paying yet?"* In his words: "I'm now in my mid sixty's, hoping to make the best of the time that I have left. I've met a wonderful lady. I now look forward to every new day. That hasn't always been the case, but I believe I'm a lucky man. There really is joy in *"A Pursuit of Life."*

To many, this book will be seen as a love story, to some possibly as a tragedy. To others the chapter titled *"Life's Lessons"* will jump out at you and to still others it will just be a real fun book to read. To the author, it was simply a way to preserve his writings until his three granddaughters would be at an age where they might develop an appreciation for them.

Once you've read this work you will find yourself picking it up time and time again just to refer back to one of the poems that was more individually meaningful. The author laughs then cries, then lives to laugh again. You will too…

A PURSUIT OF LIFE

BY:

RICHARD LEE KING

ACKNOWLEDGEMENTS

I would like to express my gratitude to Donna Chandler, for all of her help during the process of selecting which material to include and which to exclude from this work, but especially for all her editing assistance: To Judy Craddock for *insisting* that I consider *sharing* my passion with others. Special Thanks also to Diane DesRochers and Jennifer Shuster for heading me in the right direction and to Jeffery Moss for his many helpful suggestions. Thank you one and all. It never would have happened with out you.

INTRODUCTION

MY COMPUTER MATCH

I started writing poetry
long after my wife had died.
I didn't know if I could do it,
cause of course, I'd never tried.

Her passing left a hole in my world,
as you can well imagine.
Oh, I tried to carry on,
I just couldn't give it any passion.

She was really my life partner,
we shared all of our decisions.
Life seemed so much harder
under these new conditions.

I was lucky, I guess,
cause I had many a loyal friend.
Always another adventure
after each adventure would end.

And, I had several new companions,
guess I was considered a catch,
but never truly a partner,
seemed, I never met my *match*.

One day I turned in my notice,
she'd been gone for over two years.
Seemed I'd lost my motivation
and I no longer craved the *cheers*.

My boys were on their own,
they'd both moved out of state.
Finally during a month long visit
I thought I'd try to change my fate.

I packed bag and baggage,
rented out my home.
Rented from a nice young gal,
who was living all alone.

For a while I was content.
Everything was new.
Keeping your mind occupied
is the best thing you can do.

Life began to have new meaning,
I was actually having fun,
but even in my wildest dreams
I knew she was not the one.

I was nearly fifty and
she wanted to have a child.
Even in my wildest days,
I wasn't quite that wild.

We went in separate directions.
she later became a bride.
It must have been our destiny,
cause neither of us cried.

I met another lady,
it's lonely being alone.
She was really different,
liked to smoke a bone.

We spent time together,
had a lot of fun,
but I knew for the long term
she was likely not the one.

x

Her brother was my best friend,
we hung out a lot.
Even after she and I parted,
he often slept on my cot.

He became fatally ill
and during his treatment time,
she and I were together a lot
we even shared a little wine.

One thing led to another,
we got together now & then.
We both were wandering aimlessly,
down that same road again.

Those days are now long past,
water over the dam.
I still see her out sometimes,
but she's no longer in my plan.

One day on my computer,
a *"Popup"* came on my screen.
It talked about computer dating
and locals, possibly looking for me.

I never thought I'd try it,
but my interest had been peaked.
I got a **wink** from a wonderful lady
saying I might be whom she seeked.

We traded emails for quite some time,
then decided we should meet.
She suggested we go for ice cream,
so we could each take a little peek.

Now we're together often,
we like to dance at Karaoke.
Neither of us can sing,
but for us, that's *Okie Dokie*

We've gone on a cruise together
and to a wedding out of state.
We kind of looked at that,
like it was a month long date.

We just celebrated 1 full year,
we might be together to stay.
Neither of us has wavered
and we're still together today.

So, thank you computer dating,
for that popup on my screen.
It might be the first I've ever gotten
that didn't make me just want to scream.

CHAPTER ONE
THE BEGINNING

This chapter is mostly about my memories of our early life. Some of it is fabricated, but for the most part, it's as I remember things to have been. During my early childhood, we lived in difficult post depression times. However, we were not alone. It was the same for everyone and to be honest, I don't remember thinking we were any worse off than anyone else.

MY LIFE- THE BEGINNING

When I came into this life,
it was different from where I came.
I started out with nothing,
didn't even have a name.

After nine months of darkness
in a tiny 98 degree room,
suddenly it's 68 and very bright,
as I come out of the womb.

I've nothing but the air I breathe
and not a stitch of clothing.
They spank me on the butt
and that really starts me loathing.

It seems very cold
and I've not a thing to wear.
Everyone's so big
and they all have so much hair.

First this giant grabs me
and holds me by my heels.
She slaps me on the butt again,
do they know how bad that feels?

Then she hits me again,
harder by a mile.
I wonder why she did it,
did she think it would make me smile?

There are more giants all around me
and they all seem so excited.
I wonder where they came from
and were they all invited?

At first it's very scary
and they wonder why I cry.
What is this new place?
Am I about to die?

They lay me on this big ol sweaty lady
and she draws me to her breast.
Later she'll stick a nipple in my mouth,
was this some kind of test?

She had two of those things,
got so I could find them on my own.
And ya know, I grew to like em,
at that point, the best I'd ever known.

She looks like she's been through hell,
but still, she wears a smile.
I may learn to like this place,
but it just might take a while.

They call the sweaty lady Mommy.
And, Mommy seems really tired.
She thinks she's been through a lot,
but me, I'm really wired.

After the beating I just took
I just can't fall asleep,
but they give me this warm fuzzy thing,
do ya think it's mine to keep?

Everything is new
and I have so much to learn.
Everyone wants to hold me,
then they give this old guy a turn.

They're calling him my dad.
That must be his name.
He looks a lot like me.
Could our names both be the same?

Later, after Mommy falls asleep
they take me to another room.
It's filled with people more my size.
Am I part of the *baby boom?*

After a few more day's
I awaken from a nap.
Everything is moving
and I'm in my mommy's lap.

I'm searching for that nipple
and don't give me any crap.
You know I really want it
and I'm still to young to slap.

They're taking me somewhere
in something they called a car.
It's taking a long time
it must be really far.

Finally when we get there,
(I think they called it home.)
It seems much more warm and cozy,
but I find we're not alone.

There are several smaller giants,
one they call my sister.
As she stands next to Mommy,
she's so small I almost missed her.

Soon, I'll spend more time with her
and she'll turn on the charm.
But, when it comes to nipples
I prefer my mommy's arms.

There are other's they call brothers.
They all look a lot like Dad.
They must be the brother's
I never knew I had.

They all seem real friendly,
I'm beginning to like this place.
But, you should see them run
when *"up chuck"* runs down my face.

And when I messed my diaper,
you should have seen them scatter.
They all had me wondering
just what the heck's the matter?

MY LIFE - THE MIDDLE YEARS

The weeks turn into months
and eventually into years.
And, I find my early days
were the least of all my fears.

At first I can't even crawl,
but soon I learn to walk.
I listen when they move their lips
and slowly learn to talk.

My brother's teach me things.
Things city boys don't know.
Like, where babies come from
and the place where babies grow.

Every day there's something new,
it's going by so fast.
Next thing you know it's school
and Mommy wondering if I passed.

Each day's a new adventure.
So many things I've learned.
They talk about the young man
into which, I've turned.

Finally, I'm sixteen,
so I buy myself a car.
But, I still don't have my license,
so I can't drive it very far.

Next, I have a girlfriend,
she becomes my wife.
There couldn't be a better person
with whom to spend my life.

Now I have a whole new family
with another Mom & Dad.
A brother and two more sisters
to go with the one's I already had.

I'm still going to college,
working toward my degree.
I car pool with my buddy, Bill,
or sometimes he rides with me.

Soon I start a new job
I'm working for the state.
I ride to work with my brother,
so I'm almost never late.

One day Sweetie says she's pregnant,
then we have a child.
Soon we have another
and he seems a lot more wild.

We'll need a bigger house
if we're to raise these boys in style.
That means a bigger mortgage,
boy this could take a while.

First we just add on,
then the house of which she'd dreamed,
comes upon the market,
so again, we scraped and schemed.

We purchase this old farm house
with lots of vacant land.
It has a big old barn,
so one time, we brought in a band.

The house needs overhauling,
it's my brothers to the rescue.
They know just what it needs,
though I don't have a clue.

7

Our boys just love this place.
It's a great place to grow up.
There are so many things to do,
so we give them each a pup.

Life keeps passing by,
soon the boys are young adults.
We don't know how we did it,
but we both like the results.

MY LIFE - TROUBLING YEARS

Then, their mom gets sick,
struggles with her health.
If there were anything we could do
we'd spend all our meager wealth.

She puts up an admirable fight,
but the odds aren't in her favor.
You wonder how you'll make it,
was it worth those years of labor?

You wonder, am I to blame?
Was there more I could have done?
If one of us had to die,
why couldn't I have been the one?

Life is sometimes short,
you learn to take your lumps.
Another lesson learned,
it's the worst of life's speed bumps.

For a while your life is aimless,
you don't know which way to turn.
You know you're not handling things,
there's so much you've yet to learn.

You take comfort with a friend,
probably way too soon.
She's recently been divorced,
so you're singing similar tunes.

She helps you through the hard times,
you learn to smile again.
You've no idea where you're heading,
you no longer have a plan.

Somehow, life goes on,
time so quickly passes.
First you're learning to walk,
then can't see without your glasses.

MY LIFE - TODAY

Finally another generation
begins to take on its shape.
First comes sweet little Christy,
Grandmother's little namesake.

Then comes Kylie & Rachel,
they'd all make their grandma proud.
She'd have spoiled them all rotten,
if she'd only been allowed.

Now the family's all in Florida,
we all live close together.
We can help each other out
when we've hurricanes to weather.

Soon you're feeling old,
life no longer holds much fun.
You long to love again,
if you could find the perfect one.

You've been single twenty years
plus maybe a couple more.
And, every day you spend alone
makes life seem like such a bore.

You finally meet a lady
to help you pass the time.
You meet her on the internet
and so far she seems just fine.

You've only known her for a year,
but you both know the score.
And, every night you spend with her
makes you want for more.

You steal some precious moments
and look forward to many more.
You've only ever felt this way
just a couple times before.

You hope the prize is worth it
and that you can afford the cost.
Cause, with no one in your life,
you've recently felt so lost.

Life is full of unknowns.
Seldom are you sure.
But, this time you are hoping
she'll turn out to be your cure.

FAMILY

There were six of us…..plus Mom & Dad.
12 years separated the oldest from the youngest,
So, not very much camaraderie
existed amongst us.

When I was born,
Dad was in the Army in World War Two.
Later, my brother went to Korea,
my oldest son did too.

Times were tough,
but we lived on a farm
and in those days, not much you did
could cause very much harm.

There was food on the table,
but not much variety.
And, we didn't have much in common
with high society.

Most of our clothing
was hand-me-downs.
And, it wasn't very often
that we went into town.

We picked pickles for market
and chopped wood for heat.
Raised chickens for eggs.
hogs & cows for meat.

Sometimes I milked the cows
and helped butcher the chickens.
Nothin's as stinky
as wet feather pickin.

We raised a garden,
and after tilling and planting,
we pulled lots of weeds,
then came harvesting and canning.

We often went fishin'
as a family outing.
Bullheads, mosquitoes
and "be quiet no shouting."

We hunted and trapped
and fished through the ice.
We squabbled and fought,
then tried to make nice.

We didn't all make it
all the way though high school
but we were all raised
to be nobody's fool.

I was the first
to make it from High School to college.
Yet, I'm still the one
with the least amount of knowledge.

We've built cars and guarded convicts
and worked in finance.
We've worked farms and factories
and left things to chance.

We've all married & had children,
some more than others
and they're all good people,
just like my sister's and brother's.

Now we're spread out
all over this great land.
But, if one should have a need,
we'll all lend a hand.

13

I now live in Florida,
as do both of my sons.
One with two daughters
the other with just one.

Dad's been gone now
thirty years and more.
He and Mom both passed
at the age of sixty four.

From where we all started,
we've come pretty far
but we're all still family
where ever we are.

THE OLD DAYS

We walked to school,
it was a mile and a quarter.
But, you could cut cross lots
to make it a little shorter.

Winter or Summer
we made that trek.
But, we were used to it,
so what the heck.

We often shopped at *Brownie's,*
cause he let Dad charge,
but our grocery budget
was never very large.

Though my memory is dim
I know we got welfare for a while.
It's got starving to death
beat by a mile.

We raised much of our food
by planting a garden.
We all had to help out,
no one got a pardon.

We raised chickens & ducks
and the occasional goose.
Sometimes we penned them,
but mostly they ran loose.

We had a few cows,
maybe a half dozen hogs.
Vern & I would jump 'em
and ride though the bogs.

We used to cut hay,
bring it in loose.
Store it away in the mow
with some hooks on a noose.

We raised corn for the animals
cut it by hand.
I remember corn shocks standing
all over the land.

In the beginning I can remember
Dewey, our work horse, pulling a plow.
Somehow we managed,
but I don't really know how.

In the summer sometimes,
we'd go *fishin'* or *Froggin.'*
In the winter we'd slide down the hills
on a homemade toboggan.

We roamed all over the land
and built more than one fort.
Often, we'd just make up
our own kind of sport.

We made our own bow's
and used *Goldenrods* for arrows.
We made our own *slingshots*
and shot lots of sparrows.

I remember a BB gun fight
with big brother Tommy.
Vern & I against him,
I pretended he was a *Commie.*

We played *mudgutter* or *kick the can,*
but mostly *hide N seek.*
Sometimes, we'd walk for miles
to go fishin' in a creek.

16

Once, we dammed up the creek,
to make our own swimming hole,
but if we fished in it,
it was with a homemade pole.

We trapped muskrats in the winter
and caught the occasional mink.
Skinned them out in the cellar,
or sometimes in the sink.

We made bicycles from parts
salvaged from other people's junk.
We slept all in one bedroom,
sometimes two or more to a bunk.

Once, Vern swung from tree rope
and put a car in the ditch.
We used to do things like that,
just to hear *The Old Lady* bitch.

We used to swim in the Grand River
and jump from the *trestle.*
It wasn't the safest of things,
but the memories are special.

And, it was probably safer
than ole *Deuster's Dump.*
You could swim in it,
but you'd better not jump.

Our evening entertainment
was listening to radios.
The Green Hornet, The B-R-B Riders
and *Only the Shadow knows.*

We were the last in the neighborhood
to even own a TV.
It was an old used black & white,
WJIM the only channel we could see.

17

The picture was always snowy,
there was never an exception.
Dad ran two wires all around the house
trying to get better reception.

In the early days, we cut wood
with an ax and with a crosscut saw.
It didn't leave time for getting in trouble,
so we never worried about the law.

We hauled it from the woods
behind *Dewey* on an old *stone bolt*.
Later Dad bought an old tractor,
I think he got it in Holt.

We saved change in a jar up in the cupboard.
Ron put in the most, I think.
That old tractor really saved us,
brought us back from the brink.

Then dad rigged up a buzz saw
that hooked up to the front of the tractor.
And, after all those years,
Dewey was no longer much of a factor.

Later, we got a chain saw
and cutting went much faster,
but when you cut wood with Dad,
he was always *Lord and Master.*

When I was really young,
I picked up apples for 10 cents a crate.
One day I made a whole dollar,
most I'd ever made to that date.

We used to pickup beer and pop bottles
we found in the ditch.
The 2 cent deposit was the same,
it didn't matter which.

Then spend it to buy *Bugler and papers*
so we could roll cigarettes.
To a ten year old,
that's about as good as it gets.

Time's have changed
and those days are long past.
But, the memories I have,
forever will they last.

ALL ABOUT ME

I'm 16, hell on wheels,
just got my drivers license.
I hit the road bag and baggage,
ain't seen much of my home since.

I'm 19 & graduated,
wanting to do what's right…..
Thought about signing with Uncle Sam,
but I'm not looking for a fight.

Instead I'm off to college
looking for my degree,
at 21 I married my sweetheart
knowing she's in love with me.

I'm 21, legal to drink,
though it will never be a habit.
And, when I've had a few too many,
I'll either walk or cab it.

At 22, I had a son.
At 24, another.
You just can't raise a boy alone,
he has to have a brother.

By now I've hit my stride
and I've started my career.
We own a house, we're doing well,
we live without much fear.

For nearly 21 years,
I seldom miss a day,
unless it's for vacation,
or related to work some way.

Although we're not really wealthy,
we don't want for much.
We have a pretty good life
with lots of toys and such.

We buy a bigger house,
invest some for the future.
We think we've got forever,
but you never know for sure.

Time goes by, our boys grow up,
life is like we dreamed.
Then comes the *diagnosis*
and I'm nothing now, but steamed.

She fights a valiant fight,
but it's one that she can't win.
Even though we both prayed
time and time again.

Life goes on, I wander some,
but nothing seems to fit.
My life was near perfection
now I can hardly get a hit.

There've been some special ladies,
just not that perfect one.
Not that I was always looking,
sometimes it was just for fun.

But, now I'm in my sixty's
still facing life alone,
so I try online dating,
trying to avoid the phone.

Immediately I find her,
could this be my fate?
She just seemed extra special,
even before our first date.

21

Tonight we're having dinner,
we're taking that next step.
It's been planed for several days,
since then, I've hardly slept.

This story has no ending,
it hasn't happened yet,
but for my remaining days
I'll be as happy as I can get.

CHAPTER TWO
LOSING A SOUL MATE

I lost my wife to cancer shortly after she turned 40. Since then, I've spent many a lonely evening putting my thoughts down on paper. After a fashion, the hurt became more tolerable and I began to heal. I continued to record my thoughts and I've written poems covering various subjects from my childhood, to my recovery from the loss of my wife and moving beyond it to the pursuit of new meanings and new relationships. This chapter is dedicated to the memory of my loving wife Christine.

MY GIRL

For Chris

She was only fourteen when we first met,
the prettiest girl I'd seen yet.
She said no, the first time I asked
and everyone knew she had me out classed.
But, I was persistent, and after a while,
she stopped frowning at me and started to smile.
After some prodding, she finally agreed
and I swore that one chance was all I would need.

We dated until a year after she'd finished school,
then I asked if she'd be willing to marry this fool.
She hesitated, but for just a short time,
then her eyes started to twinkle, making them shine.
We had very little, except for each other,
but we knew that we'd make it one way or another.
When you start with nothing you have nothing to lose
and it gave us the freedom to live life as we choose.

We lived as paupers for those first few years,
but we learned the meaning of "Blood, Sweat and Tears."
Then, I got out of college and found better employment.
We added some class to our form of enjoyment.
We started a family, just like we'd planned.
Got a bigger house, then bought some more land.
We prospered some, though we were never rich,
but at least I wasn't digging that same ol ditch.

Then, one day we discovered that we were in trouble.
Our world was crushed and it burst our bubble.
She had a lump, which they said wasn't serious,
but before it was over we were pretty damn furious.
Doctors & hospitals and lots of medication.
Chemotherapy and rest, then finally radiation.
She fought like a trooper, but she never complained.
She didn't want her family to suffer her pain.

We weren't really religious, but we learned to pray,
hoping that a miracle just might come our way.
With all of my being I tried hard to believe,
that for someone this special, He'd grant a reprieve.
Church every Sunday, faith healers and all,
hoping that somehow, He'd answer our call.
Then as I stood there overlooking her casket,
I had a question for Him, but I never did ask it.

I no longer believe, though most think that I should.
Pray if you like, but it did us no good.
Church is a good thing for the comfort of friends.
But, upon death, I'm convinced everything ends.
Religion is for the living & if it helps you muddle through,
you have my blessing and I'm happy for you.
But, I believe that Heaven and Hell,,,, God and Jesus,
though very well intentioned, are only there to appease us.

THINKING OF CHRISTINE

It's not yet six o'clock.
I just returned from happy hour fun.
Only had a couple beers,
but my night's already nearly done.

I really want to hold her,
but it seems there's just no way.
So, I'll watch TV and think of her
just like every other day.

We were never promised easy,
we sometimes travel the bumpy road.
When I'm going through hard times,
her memory helps to ease my load.

I'd like to spend more time with her,,,,,
oh she'll visit, but she can't stay.
Though my bottle's nearly empty,
thoughts of her don't go away.

She's often all I think about,
she visits nearly every day.
We had hoped for a lifetime,
but it didn't turn out that way.

Now all that's left are memories
of a love that was tried and true.
And the memories seem to get in the way
of finding someone new.

REMEMBERING CHRISTINE

Love came to visit me,
many, many years ago.
It didn't happen over night.
It came creeping up real slow

She had all the beauty of the sun
as it rushes toward the sea.
Yet all the strength
,,,,,of that great sea
as it crashes to the land.

We thought we had forever,,,,
Forever was what we had planned....
We thought we'd still be around
when that great sea,,,,,
,,,crushed all the rocks to sand.

Was I inspired by her beauty?
Enraptured by her charm?
I don't know that it really matters,
cause she walked by my side,,,,
and we walked arm in arm.

You know those goose bumps that you get,,,,,,?
when you hear the bugler play?
Even though you might not know
whom they're taking away....?

I still get those goose bumps,,,,,
when I hear our certain songs....
And, sometimes my eyes will tear......
cause even after all these years
the feeling's are very strong.

Forever is supposed to last forever,
but not for me and mine.
No, our forever ended
the day she ran out of time.

I've struggled with that some,,,,
and with some promises I made.
But, through it all I've kept my word,
and I think she'd give me a passing grade.

She comes drifting back to me
even though I know she's gone.
And I think she thinks, (and I agree)
we've been apart too long.

Love visited me,
I took her for my bride.
Now, after all these years,
I'm nearing my last ride.

But, before I go,
I want you all to know
my heart is filled with pride,
that those of you who are yet to follow,
once stood by my side.

TALKING TO CHRISTINE

We all knew your time was coming.
In fact, I'd known for several years.
But, those first moments after it happened,
I've never known such fear.

We had danced around the subject,
unwilling to give up hope.
Then they gave you 30 days
and I felt like such a dope.

I thought I had prepared,
that I knew how I'd react.
But, the brain gets really scrambled,
when knowing turns into fact.

That day my world just crumbled.
The next few days were such a blur.
Weeks turned into months
but still, I found no cure.

During visitation, I was out of words,
but our oldest was by my side
and the way he conducted himself
made me nearly burst with pride.

It seemed he had a strength,
which must have come from you.
Everything was strange,
but he knew just what to do.

Our youngest really struggled,
but he wouldn't let it show.
He kept it bottled up inside,
he's the sentimental one, you know?

At first, I was disappointed,
but later we conversed.
The guilt that he was feeling,
he never had rehearsed.

Your Mom and Dad shared a hug
and spoke for a moment or two.
We were all so glad to see it,
even as we mourned for you.

When we gathered to say goodbye
and send you on your way,
your Mom and sisters helped me,,,
they still do, to this very day.

Our big old house felt empty,
no longer like a home
and I knew I couldn't make it,
at least not completely on my own.

Vern Gosdin may have said it best
as I listened all alone.
He said you don't know lonely
"Until it's chiseled in stone."

Your Aunt Mary and Aunt Pat
helped clear out all your things.
Sundays I'd go to church
then cry when the choir sings.

I took comfort with a friend
who seemed to understand my pain.
We dried each other's tears
and helped keep each other sane.

Somehow it didn't feel right,
your memory couldn't be replaced.
I vowed it always would be honored
and that you'd never be disgraced.

30

I moved on several times,
lovely ladies were they all.
But, love never overcame me
seemed I wasn't able to fall.

I still carry on,
though at times I wonder why.
But, our two boys still need me
and at times, I help them to get by.

I marvel at the men they've become,
knowing they share your wisdom.
And the lessons that you taught,
they still carry with them.

The oldest now has a wife.
She reminds me somewhat of you.
I know she loves her two daughters'
and I know that you would too.

The youngest also has a daughter
that you never got to know.
All three are truly little angels
and I know you'd love them so.

They all seem to care about me
and I enjoy watching as they grow.
I know they'd make you proud
and that's all I really need to know.

And so I muddle through,
as the months turn into years,
I often think of you
and still, it often ends in tears.

SHE'S ALWAYS STANDING THERE

Last week at the airport
and one day at the mall.
I've seen her nearly every day
since she answered that fatal call.

Driving down *Old Dixie*,
heading for the county fair,
thought I saw her car
up ahead somewhere.

In line to buy my ticket
thought I saw her standing there.
Who was that guy she was with?
When did she change her hair?

Saw her twice last evening
and twice the day before.
Ever since she left me,
I see her more and more.

Last week at the barber shop
waiting my turn in the chair,
looking out the window,
thought I saw her standing there.

Never does she speak,
but she knows that I still care
and every time I turn around
she'll be standing there.

Over by the elevator,,,,,
or in the Doctor's waiting chair,
seems every time I see some gal
I always see her hair.

I've heard the only cure,
when your true love has been taken,
is get out there and start again,
pretend you're not so shaken.

I've been looking every night
in my favorite neighborhood bar.
I see her lips, her face, her body
and occasionally her car.

Last night I was *fixin'* to get lucky
with a friendly neighborhood lass,
when suddenly she showed up
right there inside my glass.

She was there when I went to bed.
She was there when I got up.
She was there when I brewed my coffee,
she was right inside my cup.

I just can't get over my lost love,
cause I see her everywhere.
And every time I turn around
she's always standing there.

I DON'T BELIEVE

I don't believe in Heaven.
I don't believe in Hell.
If there's a God looking after us,
He can't be doing very well.

Oh, I've been exposed
to the teachings of Christ.
But, lately it seems,
I've had to stop and think twice.

Our country's in a shambles.
The whole world is, in fact.
How could there be a *Katrina?*
Would a God have created that?

And, what about that *Tsunami*
and all the people who died?
Seems a God would have prevented it,
or at least, He should have tried.

Earthquakes and volcano's?
Mudslides and floods?
Tornado's and hurricanes?
The world's oozing blood!

Children are starving,
yet we have billionaires.
If there were really a God,
wouldn't He equal out the shares?

If there really were a God
who was able to create.
Wouldn't you think the world
would be in a much better state?

What about the fighting and killing,
in ours and other lands.
Would a God allow it to happen,
if it were truly in His hands?

34

I don't believe in Heaven.
I've been told that that's my right.
But, if there's a God and Heaven,
why so many fights?

Since the beginning of recorded time,
there's been one war after another.
Most were over religious beliefs,
taught to us by our mothers.

If there really were a God,
He'd be a better referee.
He wouldn't allow all the wars,
fought in the name of thee.

When my wife left us,
that was His final straw.
If there really is a God,
He's got a fatal flaw.

Never, have I known someone
more deserving, every day.
If there really was a God
she'd not have passed away.

There are people far less giving
still here with us today.
This world would be a better place
if she'd have been allowed to stay.

I don't believe in God.
And, I know I have that right.
A real God wouldn't have made her suffer,
or He'd have allowed her to win that fight.

If there really were a God,
and he really could create.
He'd make better choices.
He'd not have made that mistake.

DID SHE KNOW?

One day my special one
just up and passed away.
When that day comes along
it's to late to say what you wanted to say.

Suddenly she was gone
and I realized there wasn't any more
no more hugs, no more kisses,
no one to meet me at my door.

No more intimate conversations,
no soul mate and no lover.
No one to snuggle up with,
underneath the covers.

Most often these things happen
without a lot of warning.
They're there, then they're gone
and suddenly, you're in mourning.

In her case we saw it coming,
we had a chance to say goodbye.
Still, it causes you to wonder,
am I man enough to cry?

Did she know how much I loved her?
Did she know I'd carry on?
Did she know how much I'd miss her,
after she was gone?

Were there things we should have shared,
when we knew her time was near?
Should I have been more open
about how much I lived in fear?

Do you suppose she even suspected
that twenty years after she was gone,
she'd still be in my thoughts
and I'd still be singing her song?

36

DID WE MAKE YOUR MOMMA PROUD

Twenty years …..
That's how long she's been gone.
Man, It's so hard to believe
that it's been anywhere near that long.

I wonder what she would say,
if we could talk to her now?
Would she say, I wonder,
guys you've all made me proud?

Have I lived my life
to honor her memory?
Or, have I selfishly lived
just to satisfy me?

Have I honored the promise's,
which she asked me to keep?
Does she know I still think about her,
or that sometimes, I still weep?

Would she approve of the way
I've gone on with my life?
Would she be happy, or sad,
that I haven't taken a wife?

Would it be easier for her
if she knew I still miss her?
In my dreams she's still so real,
sometimes it seems I could kiss her.

Have I been a good influence
on her children and mine?
Would we have done a better job,
if she hadn't run out of time?

She's missed more than half
of the lives of her son's.
She never met your daughters,
or your chosen ones.

Would she be proud of the lives
that the three of us lead?
Or, would she be thinking
we're not quite up to speed?

I made her a promise
that I've kept ever since,
though I often have wondered,
did I misunderstand what she meant?

Was she thinking of her dad
and the lady in his life?
Was she trying to warn me
about the dangers of a wife?

Would she be proud
of the paths our lives have taken,
or would she think, somehow
we're all sadly mistaken?

Would she be proud of the choices
that you boys have made?
Would she be as proud as me
that you both have a trade?

I know she'd be proud
of those daughters you've born,
yet I still have some questions,
I still feel a bit torn.

Have we honored her memory?
Have we done her proud?
Shouldn't we have done more for *Granny*?
Are we still under a cloud?

Life has gone on
without her, it seems,
but still I have questions
about what it all means.

I'm proud of you guys.
I think we've all stood up to the test.
But, sometimes I still wonder,
have we done our absolute best?

STILL MOURNING?

She owned the best years
of this young mans life.
In the first days I only dreamed
one day, she'd be my wife.

Then, for 20 plus years
she gave all that she had,
to give a great life
to her kids & their dad.

She taught them to live life
without having regrets.
She said we should "mourn her,
then get over it"

So, for a short time, I mourned,
then tried to move on,
yet after several new faces
she never really was gone.

Then, crowding sixty
and still on my own,
I was tired of the feeling
of being alone.

Eggs over easy,
home fries and grits,
that's about as complicated
as my breakfast usually gets.

Several days a week,
that's the order I'd place,
just hoping she'd notice
the smile on my face.

There are good ones & bad ones
and some in between,
but none that come close
to the girl still in my dreams.

Then nearing *Medicare,*
a new love I found.
She was a beautiful blonde,
whom I hadn't seen around.

We met for ice cream,
and she seemed really nice.
Should I ask her out again?
Should I roll the dice?

I'm such a fool,
this just never could be.
This beautiful blonde,
falling for me?

But, you'll never know,
if you don't take a chance
and she'd already told me
that she just loved to dance.

Next day I took her
for a convertible ride,
now wherever I go,
she'll be by my side.

We go to the *Legion,*
the *Moose* and the *"V"*
and whenever she dances
it's always with me.

She's a special lady
and If life follows my plan,
she'll share many precious moments
with her new biggest fan.

41

I'VE MET A WONDERFUL NEW FRIEND

This isn't my goodbye,
we'll still visit now and again,
but likely much less often
and I don't know just where or when.

You're still on my mind a lot,
just not every single day.
You see, I met a wonderful new friend
and she's been chasing you away.

That was never her intention,
she has memories of her own.
But, she's often on my mind
when I find myself alone.

I'm confident you'd have liked her,
that she'd have been your friend,
if things had worked out differently,
if there'd have been a different end.

She'll never get to know about
the trust we came to share,
or the loneliness we felt,
when the other wasn't there.

But, she's brought joy into my life
for the first time in quite a while
and when we spend time together
it's much easier for me to smile.

I know you'll always be there,
as will her old memories,
but together we'll seek our future
sharing whatever's on the breeze.

CHAPTER THREE
PURSUIT BEGINS

The loss of a loving spouse is much different than the loss of a close friend or even a parent. It takes much longer to recover. But, in time you do move forward. At first though, even as you move on, you still go back. This chapter is about the efforts to move on. It's about the *PURSUIT* of someone with whom to share a meaningful tomorrow.

STARTING OVER

We're no longer together.
For that, we share the blame.
Recently we spoke again,
but there's no flicker to the flame.

Oh, at times I think about her,
but we're both set in our ways.
We had some rewarding nights,
but not enough to offset the days.

We couldn't make each other happy,
neither of us willing to bend.
So, rather than punish ourselves,
we just let the relationship end.

She's gone on with her life
and I wish her all the best,
but I wonder, given another chance,
would we pass each others test?

We're still pretty good friends,
with the others best interests in mind.
Never were we rude to each other.
Neither were we ever unkind.

I sometimes miss the things we shared
though we really needed to part.
I believe I'm ready for someone new,
but I don't know just where to start.

I've thought about the internet,
maybe *shopping online*,
but I'm a bit of an introvert
and I'm afraid of what I might find.

Still, it's worked for others,
I just might give it a chance.
With luck, I'll find that special one
who'll join me for my last dance

SHE

I live life as I please.
I'm single by my own choice.
There are no disagreements,
no one ever raises their voice.

I do whatever I want,
which really isn't so very much.
Yet, I still find myself longing
for a lady's gentle touch.

She's on my mind each morning
and every evening as I lie down.
Still, life is much less complicated
when there's no *she* around.

I'm not much good with turmoil,
age may have taken a toll.
But, with no *she* in my life
it's like I have no soul.

I don't need someone looking after me,
nor someone who needs to be looked after.
I just want a *she* to have fun with
and enjoy some mutual laughter.

Someone with whom to share life
without all the complications,
have fun, frequently wake up together,
yet comfortable taking separate vacations.

But, time waits for no one,
that which remains surely won't last.
She should occasionally share my sunrise
before our time has passed.

NO ONE

I like this feeling of being free,
no one to satisfy but me.
No one to tell me when to sleep.
No one to say what hours I keep.

No one to tell me when I wake,
where to go or what to take.
No one to ask for permission to go.
No one to answer to yes or no.

No one to accuse me of playing games,
of seeing other women, or asking for names.
No one to plan with for a rainy day.
No one to get mad and turn away.

No one to tell me what I already know.
No one to say, "It's time to go."
No one to say, "You're getting fat."
No one to get mad and call me a brat.

No one to give me a bunch of flack.
No one to remind me when I'm getting slack.
No one from whom permission to seek.
No one to tell me my outlook is bleak.

No one gets mad and rants and raves.
No one gets nasty. No one misbehaves.
No one rushing me out the door.
No one to tell me they need something more.

No one to tell me about their need.
No one's mouth but mine to feed.
No one to say what games I see.
No one to answer to, no one but me.

No one's happiness to be responsible for.
No one to tell me I could be so much more.
No one complains about how much I read.
No one with whom I must beg and plead.

No one to tell me about her rights.
No one to cause more sleepless nights.
No one to say, "I don't like your song."
No one to correct me when I'm wrong.

No one to accuse me of running around.
No one to encourage me, when I'm down.
No one to tell me how badly I've failed.
No one to remind me my ship already sailed.

No one to push me to newer heights.
No one with whom to see the sights.
No one with whom to climb the peak.
No one with whom my fortune to seek.

No one to tell me that I'm up the creek.
No one to help me patch the leak.
No one to help me when it's time to bale.
No one with whom I must pass or fail.

No one to comfort when she is sad.
No one to scold me when I've been bad.
No one to wish I were more than I am.
No one to push me. No one to plan.

No one to hurt and bring to tears.
No one to call me *Honey*, or *Dear*.
No one to complain about my stinky feet.
No one to cook the food that I eat.

No one to talk to, nothing to say.
No one to ask me about my day.
No one to love. No one to fight.
No one to enjoy the things that I write.

No one to make me feel that I'm weak.
No one with whom new sights to seek.
No one to calm me when I blow.
No one to cuddle when we dance real slow.

No one with whom to visit the shore.
No one to nudge me when I snore.
No one to remind me of all that I lack.
No one to give me a pat on the back.

No one to guide me when I drink too much.
No one to soothe me with a gentle touch.
No one to whom I've promises to keep.
No one to curl up with when I sleep.

No one could make me feel this blue.
No one to say, "I still love you."
No one to comfort me when I cry.
No one to mourn me when I die.

Yes, I like this feeling of being free.
No one that I know is as happy as me.
I don't miss her, I think you can see.
Now where's the remote to my TV.

TIME TO MOVE ON

Once, I was the hammer,
I feel now more like the nail.
I need someone to be my *Jill*
to help me with my pail.

I've been *rolling with the punches*,
been *letting the sleeping dogs lie*,
been living for tomorrow,
reluctant to say goodbye.

Been down this road before
and at times, *been up the creek.*
There's temptation in this world,
but it's wisdom that I seek.

I've kept my *nose to the grindstone*,
always tried to *toe the line*,
been offered several chances,
but felt it wiser to decline.

I need someone beside me
to be *the wind that fills my sail*
and if my boat should spring a leak,
to hold my rudder while I bale.

I know what *a bird in the hand* is worth
and that *a stitch in time saves nine*,
but it's time to take some chances,
taste the more expensive wine.

I seek not fame nor fortune,
and *if push should come to shove*,
I'd want the world to know
my heart has shared your love.

RETURNING HOME

I'm in my car, heading home.
With just my thoughts, I sit alone.
She's not here, but in my heart,
never more will we be apart.

She's been in my thoughts for a very long time.
Often I've dreamt, of her lips on mine.
It could not be, or so it seemed,
could her reality exceed what I had dreamed?

I was surprised at how my comfort grew.
And, how my life feels so renewed.
A look or smile can mean so much,
sometimes maybe, just a gentle touch.

She seems to feel the same as me.
Who'd have thought that could ever be?
That I could learn to love again
or that I would love my email friend?

I thought about it as a trial run.
I only imagined it would be such fun.
She awakened something from deep within,
something I never expected to feel again.

I can't remember a kiss so sweet,
or when my life has felt so complete.
I now look forward instead of back.
I feel my life getting back on track.

I can hardly wait for her next trip South,
or, to place my lips upon her mouth.
To dance with her and go out to eat.
To say I love you and then repeat.

It may be a while before I'm able,
to put all my cards upon her table.
It could be a long, exciting wait,
but it's going to happen, cause it's our fate.

UNINVITED LOVE

As I sit here at home,
just waiting, alone,,,,,
waiting for you to <u>arrive</u>.
If you were no longer there,
or,,,,, if suddenly you just didn't care.
I wonder, would I <u>survive?</u>

I just can't figure out
how this all came about
but, I know it wasn't part of my <u>plan.</u>
How did it all come to this?
A dance and a kiss,
then all of the sudden, <u>Wham!</u>

I didn't plan to fall for you.
I was just looking for fun things to do.
That was what I thought we had <u>found.</u>
Next thing you know
where ever I would go
I wanted to have you <u>around.</u>

Although our lives had both been hexed,
I dreamed someday we'd have sex.
But, falling in love wasn't part of my <u>plan.</u>
One day I awoke and I knew
I had fallen for you,
when all I wanted was to hold your <u>hand.</u>

And what impress's me so,
just in case you didn't know,
is that it seems that you love me <u>too.</u>
The next question, I guess,
is probably,,,,,, more or less,
now what are we going to <u>do?</u>

PRECIOUS MOMENTS

I so look forward
to stolen moments in time.
Just those few precious moments
when you become mine.

A short ride in a convertible,
meeting friends at the *Boardwalk,*
or any other occasion,
when we just sit and talk.

A night of dancing
to karaoke at the *Moose.*
Getting up on the dance floor,
beginning to cut loose.

A trip to restaurant
with you and your Mom,
or those frequent messages
over internet dot com.

The condo picnic,
or a meal from our *bible.*
I'd like to lose some weight
but I guess I'm not very liable.

A trip to Michigan
for your daughter's wedding.
Buying a new suit
and doing all that fretting.

Twenty five cent drafts,
learning a new country dance,
enjoying our life,
never passing up a chance.

Then a trip to the river
to stay with some friends.
Feelings no guilt,
hoping this never ends.

Time spent in the casino
donating to the tribe.
Knowing we won't win
unless there's someone to bribe.

A broken shoe
as we were playing the slots.
Heading out early,
like it or not.

Introductions to family,
needing a dish to pass.
Heading back home,
after having a blast.

They're only memories,
both yours and mine.
,,,,,Precious moments,
,,,,,,frozen in time.

YOU'RE THE REASON I GO ON

I've been writing you some poems,
just a few words I'd like to share.
I sometimes send them to you
so you'll know how much I care.

Some are just for me,
they aren't that well written,
but others I send to you
because you've got me smitten.

You're *the straw that stirs my drink,*
the light that shows my way.
You're the sunshine in my life.
You brighten every single day.

I look forward to our time together,
whatever the occasion.
You only need to ask me once.
I don't need much persuasion.

You're the reason I can hardly wait
for each new day to start.
You're *the nourishment for my soul,*
the pump that feeds my heart.

You're the reason I go on,
the match that lights my fire.
And, every time I think of you
I'm filled completely with desire.

CHAPTER FOUR
GOING BACK HOME

I was born and raised in Michigan, however several years after my wife passed away and with both of my sons, by then living in Florida, I made the decision to give it a try. That was nearly 20 years ago. I still go back for annual visits, but Florida is now my home. This chapter attempts to address some of my feelings about those trips back home.

YEARNING FOR MICHIGAN

I packed my bags and moved to Florida
nearly 20 years ago.
Now days I often reminisce
about that life I used to know.

As great as I find these winters,
it's still so easy to say,
I miss the warming breeze in Michigan
along about the first of May.

I miss the changing of the seasons,
apple blossoms in the spring
and the greening of the grass,
as the birds begin to sing.

I miss that feeling of cleanliness
resulting from every early spring shower,
the sense that there's a newness
and the scent of all the flowers.

I miss the loveliness of lilacs
and the smell of cherry blossoms,
the sight of pussy willows
and watching for that first robin.

I miss the farmers tilling the soil
after the frost has left the ground
and the feeling of new beginnings,
which seem to be happening all around.

Then, as the year progresses,
I miss the smell of new mown hay,
the music that the birds would make
as we start another new day.

Come spring, every thing turns green,
then comes June and then July.
Many of the fields turn golden
until they combine the wheat and rye.

Soon it's high school football,
then maybe Indian Summer,
but February & March are coming,
lordy, lordy what a bummer.

I miss the changing of the leaves
and the variety of different "seasons,"
but if you wonder why I left
months 2 and 3 were my biggest reasons.

If a Michigan year was 10 months long
and I could chose which months to lose
February and March
would be the months I'd choose.

You're nearly through the football season,
you've already hunted deer,
you've enjoyed your Christmas snow
and ushered in another new year.

You've seen all the college bowl games,
you're looking forward to the *Super Bowl*,
now comes February and March
to drain your very soul.

Finally, along comes April,
the grass actually starts to green,
the snow has now all melted
and replenished every stream.

Soon the golf course beckons
and the grass needs to be mowed.
At times it's really warm,
but as a whole its still quite cold.

We're back to where we started
when I first reminisced.
Pretty much we've covered
most all those things I've missed.

I now live in paradise
with no plans for a permanent return,
but each and every spring
my heart still seems to yearn.

A TRIP TO THE RIVER

I took a trip to Michigan,
cause there's family I wanted to see.
I don't see them very often
and they mean so much to me.

I have friends on the *Muskegon river*.
They'd invited me to come and stay.
They said the more the merrier,
just come up and play.

So I invited Mom and Karen,
it was a chance for them to get away.
Mom didn't go, but Karen did
cause I wouldn't let her have her say.

When we arrived at the Clifton house
we enjoyed a friendly greeting.
Maggie's a great cook, so naturedly,
it wasn't long til we were eating.

We played a few new games.
Games we hadn't played before.
But, when the games were over
I think we were ready for more.

We were on our way to visit my sister,
when we decided Steve should drive.
He was getting familiar with the gauges,
but we were lucky to survive.

As we traveled down that road,
WOO! WOO! WOO! Karen said.
If she'd have said it a little later
I feel certain we'd all be dead.

He'd wandered over the center line
and a truck was coming fast.
He'd made a big mistake,
we're lucky it won't be his last.

Somehow it all worked out,
we arrived safely at our destination.
We made it to sis's place,
a small part of my very best vacation.

Dinner at the Big Apple,
then one of the games we'd learned.
Karen won the first game,
then she intentionally tried to get burned.

On the way back to the river,
we played games with a local sweetie.
We had stopped at the reservation,
but I don't think their honoring the treaty.

After our *donation* to the tribe
we were on the road again.
We saw several bunches of deer,
but I couldn't tell you where or when.

Next day, our hosts took us *down the river.*
(That's the *Clifton's* not the Indians.)
Then the very next day,
we did it all again.

We sat out by the camp fire
and drank whatever came along.
We listened to great music
trying to guess who sang the song.

Then, another trip down the river,
with new people we'd just met.
As far as I'm concerned
this was a good as it could get.

Later sparkling wine,
then a little coconut rum.
I couldn't remember ever a time
having this much fun.

Saturday evening the *Craddocks* arrived
I think it was sometime after eight.
It's so nice that they could join us
even though it was getting late.

My four oldest and dearest friends,
all together at one time.
Better and more trusting friends,
I expect never again to find.

At noon the very next day,
we're on the road back home.
I'll make that trip again some day,
but hopefully, I'll never make it alone.

MY BROTHER

Vern & Shirley have always been there.
How do I show them, how much I care?

Each time I go home they go out of their way,
to insure that each time, I have another great stay.

Vern was my idol, when I was a lad,
he had all of the talent that I never had.

Even in grade school, he always excelled,
but when it came to sports, I really smelled.

He was my protector and more than one time,
to save my bacon, he put his on the line.

I remember one day on my way home from school,
he took on two brothers,,, man was he cool.

They said, "Our brother will be looking for you."
Vern smiled and said, "We've got brothers too."

One year we hoed weeds and I learned to smoke.
For the first time in my life, I wasn't always broke.

When he was in high school & I was still a kid,
he often included me in things that he did.

Whenever he took me to the places he went,
who's money do you suppose it was that I spent?

He was my hero on the baseball team.
Four years he played, I could only dream.

Suddenly he's married, to some girl that he met.
Even then, his little brother, he didn't forget.

When I met Chris, a year or two later,
the way they took to her, made me want to date her.

Shirley and she, became best of friends,,,,
the kind of friendship, that just never ends.

One time we went camping in my little black bug.
camped in the road and gave our Aunt Rose a hug.

Went up on the dunes at about 5 a.m.,
scorched hell out of our feet coming down again.

Drove down this highway, which turned into a path.
Went to the Platt River, to take ourselves a bath.

Two up front, two trying to sleep.
Two big guys in that little back seat.

Canasta, Pinochle and Michigan Rummy.
Played 3 handed, or using a dummy.

Three of us played, leaving one to drive,
somehow we managed to stay alive.

I miss those days, but I did discover,
there's no better friend, then my big brother.

He's always been there for me, one way or another,
but I'd kick his fanny in golf if I had my druthers!

THANKS VERN & SHIRLEY

Once again I owe you two
for another perfect vacation.
Well, except for playing golf
and all of that aggravation.

You always take me to dinner
and I always eat so well.
Once, with a friend in Jackson
then another time in Hell.

And lets not forget Olivet,
then over in Mason at Drabs.
The Picket Fence at the lake,
boy I should be watching my *carbs.*

I know it's not your fault,
but I added another 10 pounds.
Guess I should expect that to happen
when we're out making the rounds.

When I come back to Michigan,
it's so nice to have you there
and if you'd agree to a trip to Florida,
I have a room you two can share.

My place isn't as nice as yours,
but at least the sheets are clean
and we've got some of the nicest restaurants
a body's ever seen.

We also have some *greasy spoons*
or should that be *puke -n- choke?*
We've places overlooking the water
where you can just sit & have a coke.

We've lots of courses to play,
if that should be your desire,
or we could sit on a lovely beach,
or in my back yard by a fire.

Anyway, I'd like to thank you both
for all your generosity.
For putting me up, furnishing clubs
and for having the card party.

MY MICHIGAN VACATION

It was my lengthiest vacation,
much longer than the rest.
I'd say my most enjoyable,
by far the very best.

Never was I bored,
I never longed to be back home.
Never did I miss the time
I usually spend at home alone.

First I went to Vern & Shirley's,
then my moms for a little stay.
I was there for the big celebration
taking place on Independence Day.

We were playing cards one night
when the "kids" called one after the other.
Seems there was a tornado warning
and they insisted we take cover.

Then the night before the party
Joel & Keith took time to tap the keg.
They offered me a drink,
and didn't even make me beg.

Of course, we had to test the brew,
make sure it was safe to drink.
If someone were to get sick from it,
what would people think?

We gave it a thorough testing.
Tested it time & time again.
Testing can be a difficult job
every now and then.

Karen's family all made the party,
it was a real great get together.
With lots of fun and games
and some real fantastic weather.

Glendon & Danielle were there
along with little EJ.
They have a new puppy dog,
but I don't think he was there that day.

Jim & Lisa came, although Jim
didn't last for very long.
He was drinking some weird concoction
and I think he mixed it wrong.

Mom and I played Karen and Uncle Cal
in the age old game of horse shoes.
It was a difficult game for the ladies,
but Uncle Cal wasn't about to lose.

Then there was this game Tad had built
that went over really great.
It was hard to get the hang of it,
sort of like drinking water from a plate.

He called the game *Corn Hole*
if my memory serves me right.
The game was very popular,
we played it half the night.

But, Tad's wife, Amy
made winning so much harder.
That is unless you were lucky enough
to wind up with her for your partner.

She carried me through several games
against some real tough competition.
And, Uncle Cal seemed very jealous
that he didn't wind up in my position.

Nearly everyone, except for me,
brought a dish to pass.
But, something that somebody brought
gave somebody gas.

There was pool time for all the kids,
including Daniel, Joci and Tyler.
I wasn't paying close attention,
but I think EJ even was in for a while.

Joel left the party early,
seems he took a little ride.
I couldn't drink enough to stay with him,
but you gotta' know I tried.

After all the games were played
came the culmination.
A really great fire works display
to top off the celebration.

Still later, we gathered round the fire
to discuss the days events,
but I guess we'd all petered out
before Tad made it to his tent.

Somehow, Karen didn't make it
to see Lacy clear the table.
I know she wanted to help,
she just wasn't physically able.

From the reports I got next day
Lisa, Tad & Keith tended the final flames.
The rest of us all wimped out,
probably worn out from all the games.

Next day we were heading for the river,
but Mom wasn't up to making the trip.
So, I pressed the issue with Karen,
told her not to give me any lip

You need some time away
to re-charge your battery.
There's no one you'd be safer with,
than you will be with me.

It took a little convincing,
but she finally agreed to go.
She made my trip more enjoyable
that's what I'd like for her to know.

Sunday we returned,
then I went back to see my brothers,
but the best part of my trip,
was the time spent at my mother's.

CHAPTER FIVE
LIFE'S LESSONS

I'm not really much of a philosopher, but this chapter contains some thoughts that I wanted to share with my two sons and my three granddaughters.

RAISING KIDS

Give them your love
and it comes back to you.
Give them hate
and that comes back too.

Teach them to lie
and they'll learn to steal,
but truth and honesty
have much more appeal.

Controlling our anger
is a hard lesson to learn.
'Cause it needs a proper release,
or it will simmer & burn.

Having good manners
and being polite,
beats being aggressive
and wanting to fight.

So, kill them with kindness,
teach them not to be wild
and to remember the manners
they learned as a child.

Teach them respect
and about getting along.
Make them aware
being disrespectful is wrong.

Send them to school,
then off to college.
One of your greatest gifts
is to bless them with knowledge.

Teach a good work ethic,
teamwork and ambition
and all of their dreams
might come to fruition.

Faith, hope & happiness
go hand in hand.
All things combined,
they might rule the land.

DADDY'S WORDS

Daddy was a good old boy,
wise way beyond his years.
He rode me hard throughout my life
caused a small river full of tears.

But, he tried to teach me right from wrong,
I just didn't know til' after he died.
And, if I didn't learn from him,
it wasn't cause he never tried.

Daddy's words contained a message
way more important than any song.
Daddy wanted the whole wide world
just to learn to get along.

Daddy said, "There's a time to fight,
and a time to walk away.
The wise man knows the difference.
the foolish, nearly always stay."

He said, "You only fight to save,
you never fight to prove.
If you fight for any other reason,
it's likely a very foolish move."

Daddy said, "The smartest might be right,
but the toughest usually wins most fights.
Course it really doesn't matter much,
they'll read you both your rights."

He said, "Fighting doesn't prove a thing,
win, lose or draw.
If I'm the toughest, but you are right,
wouldn't you rather draw for longest straw?"

Daddy's words come back to me
now that I'm full grown
and I'd like to pass his message on
to a couple boys of my own.

If they could hear my daddy's words,
if I could put them in a song,
maybe then they'd know there's honor
in just learning to get along.

Then, Daddy's lessons taught,
would again be lessons learned.
And I think,,,, way down deep,,,,
that's what Daddy always yearned.

YOU'RE STILL NEEDED

I've tried to live my life
so that one day you'd both say,
"If I could pick any one as my father,
I'd have picked you every single day."

Your granddad would be one hundred.
Your momma? Almost sixty five.
And, I'm sure our world would differ,
if they both were still alive.

Life didn't work out that way,
so it does little good to ponder,
but if Dad had lived to teach me,
would things have differed, I wonder?

Would his words of wisdom,
when I might have needed correction,
better have prepared me
to push you in the right direction?

And, if you hadn't lost your mom,
when still just in your teens,
you'd both have all her wisdom,
at least, to me that's how it seems.

Still, I guess we're quite lucky,
there are some in dire straits.
So far, we've been able to handle
anything heaped upon our plates.

We always pull together
whenever there's a need.
It's much thicker than water,
this family blood we bleed.

So during these troubled times,
in our struggle to survive,
try to keep in mind we're fortunate,
cause at least we're still alive.

You are both still needed,
you're not to the end of your line.
You've both still more to give
though I'm running short on time.

One day you'll be looking back
at those bringing up your rear.
I hope you'll be as proud of them
as I was of you, while I was here.

BAD DAYS *(For Karen)*

Heard about the accident,
sounds to me like another mess.
Another one of those bad days,
would also be my guess.

You've had more than your share,
of the bad ones I'd say,
those when you're called upon
to save another day.

Bad days are the speed bumps
in our life long road.
The one's you have to get over
if you're to get to the gold.

You've always kept the faith,
throughout thick and thin.
Now you're being called upon
to do it once again.

You've always been the muscle
holding everything together.
However big the storm,
you've allowed them all to weather.

You've spent your whole life
being every one else's glue.
It's important you keep believing
good days are awaiting you.

You need to trust me now
and believe me when I say,
life still holds for you
the sweetest judgment day.

Take comfort in that,
cause I'm pretty darn sure,
this was just one more test
you were meant to endure.

We just have to know,
when the final tally is done,
every test we've passed
is another battle won.

When you finally find the gold
at the end or your rainbow,
they'll fit you with a halo
and your soul will be aglow.

IF IT WEREN'T FOR BOOZE

(My buddy's best buddy is booze.)
For my friend.

My buddy and I were talking, and having a couple drinks.
Later I wrote down, all the things I think he thinks.
The words won't be exact, cause that was not my purpose.
His words had more meaning, than appeared on the surface.
Some of the things he said, probably shouldn't be repeated,
but mostly, someone to talk to was all he really needed.

He said,

"If it weren't for booze,
I'd still be spending my life with her…..
and she'd be dressed to the teeth in diamonds and fur.
I'd still own a car and I'd still have a house
and I wouldn't feel like the worlds biggest louse.
I wouldn't have lost everything I had to lose
and I'd still have her,
                              If it weren't for booze…"

I wouldn't always have to be walking to work.
I'd have fewer reasons to feel like a jerk.
"I wouldn't have to live so close to my job
and she wouldn't think that I'm such a slob.
              ,,,,,If it weren't for booze… "

"There'd have been food in the fridge & money in the bank
and I wouldn't have spent so many nights in the tank.
She wouldn't have had to come up with bail
to get my drunk fanny out of that nasty ol jail.
              ,,,,,If it weren't for booze…"

"Things wouldn't be so cloudy,
my future would be looking bright,
if only I hadn't been out drinking,,,,, nearly every night.
I'd be living with her on our own private ranch,
instead of back here begging her for one more chance.
                ,,,,,If it weren't for booze..."

"She'd still be my homecoming queen,
and we'd still be writing the final scene.
We'd have seen most of the sites we were planning to see
and I'd still be her star, like I used to be.
.....The stud in her life,,,,, would still be me.
                ,,,,,If it weren't for booze."

THE REASONS MY BUDDY DRINKS
For that same good friend

When the troubles in his life
seem to have overflowed his cup.
When he thinks he can't go on,
or he's thinking of giving up.

When it all begins to bore him,
or his burden seems too great.
When it seems too many troubles
have been heaped upon his plate.

When it seems the road's too hard
or the hill's a bit too steep.
When a troubled mind is bothering him
and he's not getting any sleep.

When all the world around him
seems to be a mighty mess.
When the answers seem to escape him
and he doesn't even have a guess.

When trouble seems to surround him,
and there's no way to turn it about.
When he just wants to escape,
but there's no way of getting out.

When he knows how much he's needed,
but feels he's nothing left to give.
When he thinks his number's up
and he's not sure he wants to live.

When it seems the best solution
might just be to end it all.
When he remembers that without him,
maybe no one would answer the call.

When he thinks about those who depend on him
to answer for their needs.
When he wonders where they'd be
if not for all of his good deeds.

It could be his grand parents,
His parents, or his wife.
It could be a grandchild, or the child
to whom he's given life.

Possibly a good buddy,
an uncle, or an aunt.
When he thinks of all he's given,
that other people can't.

He thinks of his love for sweetie
and of her love for him.
It's brought him back from the depths
time and time again.

When it seems he's always struggling,
but he's steadily losing ground,
or he thinks about the mess they'd be in,
if he just weren't around.

When the world just isn't his oyster,
or it seems life's not his cup of tea,
he thinks of the affect he's had
on the likes of folks like me.

He knows that life goes on,
and probably they'd survive,
but who'd be there to guide them,
if he no longer were alive?

He remembers there are consequences
to all we do or say.
Without him in their lives,
it'd all turn out a different way.

82

Then, after he's thought it through
and sorted out all the junk,
he finds his only solution
is to go out and get stinking drunk.

Of course, if you're a religious man,
that might not be your way.
So, after you get good & *snockered*,
you might get on your knees and pray.

Still, when all is said and done
and everyone's had their say,
the sun will come up tomorrow
and we'll start a brand new day.

PATRIOTIC POETRY

I've always been a saver.
That's always been my curse.
Sometimes the things I save
are other peoples' verse.

These are from my Patriotic Collection,
they've spoken to my heart.
I pass them on to you
just trying to do my part.

Often I write poems,
or for me, what passes as such,
but I don't have the skills
to write so little, yet say so much.

These all need to be seen,
we need to pass them around.
Our country would really benefit
if more patriotism could be found.

They all came from the internet,
probably written by hand,
most by one of our soldiers
stationed in some foreign land.

Some address facing their maker,
they all speak to your heart.
Mostly they're all very proud
just knowing they've done their part.

Some talk about the conditions,
some comparing them to hell,
but our country's in good hands,
from their words it's easy to tell.

They talk of burdens born,
of honor and of pride.
A 21 gun salute,
as a friend takes that final ride.

I'm betting you can't read them
without shedding several tears,
but trusting in our soldiers
should calm most all our fears.

I hope that you'll enjoy them,
that you'll also pass them along.
It's time we all showed more pride
and played more patriotic songs.

JUST 'CAUSE THE CAUSE IS JUST

I had seven or eight poems
I was wanting to pass along.
Most were written by our soldiers,
by the way, they're holding strong.

But, it was *suggested* that I shouldn't,
that lawsuits might ensue,
even though the only motive was
getting those patriotic thoughts to you.

We need to support our troops
that really seems to be a must.
The only reason they are there,
is just 'cause the cause is just.

We need to be more vocal
in defending what is right.
The squeaky wheel gets noticed,
we should squeak, with all our might.

We have lots of vocal fanatics
spouting all sorts of crap,
but last time I checked USA
was still atop my country's map.

We need more people standing up
for what they know is right.
We need to show the enemy
they just can't win this fight.

We need to show more resolve,
stop talking about pulling out.
Remember 9-11?
That's what it's really all about!

I'm really not political,
but I know that right is right
and knowing that the troops are there
helps me sleep at night.

For over two hundred years
we kept foreign battles from our shores,
but ever since 9-11
we can't say that anymore.

Oh I know, we fought amongst ourselves
when we fought that *civil war,*
but that was a hundred fifty years ago
we shouldn't fight ourselves anymore.

Our soldiers all salute our flag,
they've all shared the costs.
Once they've worn the uniform
seems, that respect is never lost.

We can't right all the wrongs,
but we need to do the proper thing
and when they play our National Anthem
we all need to stand <u>and</u> sing.

To those who are too embarrassed,
or who just don't feel the pride,
there are borders north and south,
we should offer them *another free ride.*

It's not about religion, but if it is,
that religion just can't be right.
The flag's been there since 1776,
we've already fought and won that fight.

I don't have the answers,
but I know we all need to unite
and I know this talk of pulling out
doesn't increase our soldiers might.

IT'S NOT MY JOB

It's not my job to fight the war,
nor did I declare it.
But, the freedom that it brings,
well I certainly want to share it.

It's not my job to train the troops
nor even to recruit them.
But, for the job that they all do,
I certainly do salute them.

It's not my job to arm the soldier,
I'm not in uniform.
But I can & must show my support,
as they so expertly face the storm.

It's not my job to fly the planes,
nor do I drive the tanks.
But, all of those who do,
deserve their entire country's thanks.

It's not my job to be a warrior.
I may not be that brave,
but I have humbly bowed my head
at many a warrior's grave.

It's not my job to protest,
while lives are being lost.
Nor to mock the freedom,
which comes at such great cost.

Ours is the greatest country,
we look out for all the rest.
And, it's partially that sense of duty,
which makes us the all time very best.

It's my job to honor my country
and in every way I can,
to stand behind her soldiers
and fall inline behind the plan.

If I can't do my job,
it might be time for me to leave.
To find another country
in whose constitution I believe.

GOD BLESS AMERICA
EARTHS WATCH DOG
LAND OF THE FREE
HOME OF THE BRAVE
AND THE SITE OF MANY A
BRAVE WARRIORS GRAVE

CHAPTER SIX
FOR MY MOM

Other than your wife, your children and their children there is no one more meaningful in your life than your mom. My mom passed away years ago and I adopted my mother-in-Law as my new *mom*. This chapter is entirely to, for and about her. She is such a special person.

MOM'S CHRISTMAS POEM - 2005

Well, it's Christmas time again,
seems time goes by so fast.
Your working on a Halloween costume
then suddenly, Thanksgiving's already past.

I keep telling myself one of these days,
I'll spend another Christmas in the snow.
I've even shopped for a ticket,
just can't work up the courage to go.

Cold and I just don't agree,
sunshine's what I really like.
Besides, if I were to come up there,
I'd need mud & snow tires for my bike.

But, when the holidays are over
and I've broken all my new years resolutions,
when the weather's warm and the flowers bloom,
I'll come up with a better solution.

On Christmas day we'll think of you
and we'll all wish that you were here.
Unfortunately, we'll just have to settle
for a Christmas toast with holiday cheer.

CHRISTMAS - M0M, 2001

Well, Christmas is here,
but you are not.
Another Christmas without you,
that's what we've got.

We all know you're grieving,
but please,,, don't grieve alone.
It's a proven fact grieving is sunshine
is less stressful than in that snow.

I'm pretty sure I know
what you're going through.
In fact, I'm pretty sure,
I went through it too.

Sometime it takes a while,
to be comfortable alone,
but once you finally get there,
you may find joy you've never known.

There'll be no one to wait on,
to pickup after as you clean.
No one will get mad,
at things you didn't mean.

There'll be no one to bitch at
and no one bitching at you.
And, no permission is needed
for things you want to do.

And, no matter what they say
about two living cheaply as one.
I'm here to tell you Mom,
it just can't be done.

There is one real plus,
if you consider it such,
you can come visit us
and it won't cost so much.

We have a place for you
and the costs are very reasonable.
You're so close to everything,
it makes it really feasible.

You can stay for a week,
a month, or the entire season.
You can do what you want.
You don't need to have a reason.

We'll all go to the beach,
or maybe get liquored up.
'Cause, nobody really cares
what's in your coffee cup.

And if you'd like to go visit
those people out west,
it's your decision,
cause *Mom* always knows best.

I'll take you to the airport.
I'll be there when you return.
Learning to enjoy your life
is your only lesson left to learn.

TO MY MOM

As my mind takes me back
to all the times that we've shared,
I realize how poorly I've been
at showing how much I cared.

You have always been there
to lend us all a hand.
First to offer encouragement,
first to show you understand.

Yet, somehow you're always last
to accept our gratitude.
Whenever we try to thank you,
seems you always *cop an attitude*.

I guess I didn't do the best of jobs
at bringing up my sons.
But, when it comes to carrying on
I know they will be the ones.

They'll make us proud, I know they will,
thanks in no small part to you.
The lessons that you taught to them,
show in all they say and do.

When it's time to step to the fore
and for them to carry on,
I'll know that much of what they do,
came directly from my *mom*.

FOR MOTHER'S DAY

Another Mothers Day has rolled around.
Seems the months go by so fast.
You're looking forward to a special occasion,
next thing you know, it's already past.

We're all doing swell,
but we really miss you a lot.
And, it's really hard playing euchre
with just the seven we've got.

I suppose Tim or I
should get ourselves a mate.
Then we'd be able to play,
cause then we'd have all eight.

No! Hold it! That's a bad idea,
I think we better wait.
Until' Chad gets a little older,
or you move to our state.

As for Timbo and Christy,
They're both doing just fine.
She stays with him quite often
and they while away their time.

You probably didn't know it,
but he finally bought the place.
And, if his renter ever moves,
he'll have an abundance of space.

Then there's Kylie and Rachael,
they're both growing so fast!
Every time I turn around,
seems another birthday has past.

And as for Kevin & Shelly,
they still like to sing.
So, most every Friday night
we're all doing their thing.

And as for Tim's and my love life,
we're both still very single.
But, last time they were singing,
seemed, he started to mingle.

He's handling it very well,
or so that's how it seems.
But, I think he's still hoping to meet
that girl who owns his dreams.

Me? I'm happy with life
just the way it is, for now.
I don't mind buying the milk,
it's having to live with the cow.

Kathy and Mike?
They seem to be doing just fine.
Nobody is always happy,
but they seem to be, most of the time.

That big ole A frame?
It's really starting to take shape.
Mike should have an 'S' on his chest
and wear a big red cape.

We had a pool for the Kentucky Derby,
probably the first bet Chad ever made.
But, when the race was all over,
take a guess at who got paid?

Anyway, you're in all of our thoughts
on a daily basis.
And, always you are with us,
at all our drinking places.

MOM'S SPECIAL DAY

Your special day is coming,
I know you're looking for a poem.
But, I bought this little card,
'cause, I'm so far away from home.

I'm sending my best wishes
and another thought or two,
cause my list of favorite people,
just happens to include you.

Haven't heard about your trip,
here's hoping that you won.
But, even if you didn't
I'd bet you had lots of fun.

I spoke with your lovely daughter,
about the Indian's scalping white's.
But, it's not about your hair,
they want lots of losing nights.

I'm sure you did your part
to contribute to their cause.
It's about the most fun that you can have
without breaking any laws.

Though I can't be there Sunday,
I sent this card to say,
I hope you and the entire family share
a very special *Mother's Day*.

A MOTHER'S DAY POEM – FOR MOM

A *mom* is someone special,
that's what you've always been.
Always trying to be helpful,
in any way you can.

A *mom* is one who cares,
for any and for all.
Always trying to be there,
to help us when we fall.

You've been a *mom* completely
for nearly all your life.
It's now time you concentrated
on just being your husband's wife.

Your kids are all full grown
and able to survive.
It's time you and your chosen
started feeling more alive.

Once, you had it started,
you traveled far and near.
How long, I wonder now,
since you've even had a beer?

You'll always be our *mom*,
we'll always love you best.
Now it's time we stand on our own,
and pass or fail the test.

A *mom* completes her *duty*
when we all come of age.
Bob Seger may have said it best,
it's time to *"turn the page."*

MICHIGAN TRIP - *Mom's birthday*

I went to visit *Mom & Karen*
to celebrate *Mom's* birthday.
The plan: While I was there,
we'd all go north to play.

They met me at the airport,
just a couple minutes late.
It's a lesson for them both,
don't let *Calvin* navigate.

We headed for the *Soaring Eagle*
to give the Indians a try.
We wanted to win some cash,
a little extra to get us by.

When we got to *Mt Pleasant*
and were driving through the town,
it suddenly occurred to us
we didn't know our way around.

We considered asking for directions,
but thought we could *muddle through*.
Of course, Uncle Cal was driving
and that's what all men usually do.

As Karen called the *Clifton's,*
we finally spotted the signs.
So, she told them, "We'll be there,
just give us a little more time."

We'd barely walked through the door,
when we noticed this big crowd.
The *Tigers* playoff game was on
and they were getting pretty loud.

Two outs in the ninth inning,
in a 3 run, all tie game.
2 men on, *Ordonez* batting,
when he added to his fame.

He hit one out and the crowd went nuts
for a 3 run *walk off homer*.
Now we're in the *SERIES*
and everybody's going *Gomer*.

We met up with the *Clifton's*
and had a little lunch.
Then we headed to the machines
hoping we'd all win a bunch.

The Indians weren't very friendly,
luck hadn't been on our side,
but *Mom and Karen* decided
there was a machine they hadn't tried.

When it was nearly time to leave
I heard a familiar *cackle*.
It sounded like they'd been attacked,
so I looked for someone to tackle.

Well, it turned out to be laughter,
cause they'd hit a lucky seven.
By the time I finally found them,
they were both in seventh heaven.

They cashed their ticket, celebrated
and we headed for the door.
Mom tucked away her winnings
and didn't think about it anymore.

Come Sunday afternoon, as she
was looking for her cash,
we all became concerned,
cause she couldn't find her stash.

An all out search ensued,
we looked in every nook and cranny.
We were sure it would turn up.
It's sometimes that way with *Granny*.

After everything was checked,
we checked everything again.
We felt it would be found,
but we didn't know just when.

She swore us both to secrecy,
made us promise not to tell.
We both thought she'd soon find it
so we both said, "What the hell?"

Well, it all ended happy,
if you can call it such.
She had hid it in the *Imodium AD*,
cause she uses it so much.

When I walked into the room
she frowned a little, but then!
She burst out in laughter,
kinda like getting 7's once again.

And that promise she made us make
we might as well never made.
Cause now Granny tells the story,
and she tells it all her way.

On our return journey,
we dropped Cal at his motor home.
It's a real nice summer setup
with lots of space to roam.

Tuesday I took Karen to work,
so we could have her car.
Thought *Mom* had a doctor appointment
and we'd have lunch at the bar.

Turned out I had the days mixed up
so we went to the dollar store.
We had a *drive up* lunch,
then I picked Karen up at four.

Wednesday was *Mom's* appointment,
so we borrowed Karen's car again,
After the trip to the doctor
we headed North, and then,,,,,,

Mom & I went to the cemetery
to clean up the family plot.
We argued about the route,
 seems we do that a lot.

We met Cal & Pat for lunch,
then argued about a name.
Now there's a dollar bet
neither of us will ever claim.

She says, "The name was Kathy."
I say, "It had an R."
We argued about it some,
but it didn't get us very far.

Usually when Karen went to work
Mom & I played *Gin*.
She beat me a couple times,
then she laid down and let me win.

I even have a score sheet
I'm planning to put in a frame.
I think it's called a *skunk*
when you win a scoreless game.

Later in the week, I came in
and caught *Mom* exasperated.
She couldn't find the TV remote
and she was rather agitated.

She had tried to change the channel
using the cordless phone.
Later, she discovered
the remote had a brand new home.

There was a dinner at Tad & Amy's,
they're *black sheep* Spartan fans.
So, *Maze & Blue* footprints
became a part of my plans.

They have a beautiful new home
with a basement party room.
It's dedicated to *Green & White*
with no room for *Maze & Blue*.

It was a very restful trip
with the occasional happy hour.
I couldn't have enjoyed it more
had we visited the *Eiffel Tower*.

Back home in *Florida,*
I received a telephone call.
Seems *Mom* had received a package
that proves she bared it all.

She knows Steve & Maggie well,
but she doesn't know their game.
They both enjoy a good joke
as long as there's no shame.

Seems she'd left her *"undies"*
under Steve & Maggie's bed.
She thought they'd throw them out,
but they showed up in her mail instead.

HAPPY BIRTHDAY MOM - 2005

I can't remember the last time
we were together on *your* day.
And, I know you'd rather forget it,
but HAPPY BIRTHDAY anyway.

We're all so happy that you're here
for your Libra indoctrination.
We'll party til the sun comes up,
cause you can heal during your vacation.

Today you get to make a fool of yourself,
without any fear of reprisal.
And, if you think your head might suffer,
the *hair of the dog* helps to insure survival.

When you add up all your birthdays,
it comes out to lots of celebrations.
But, wouldn't you rather have it that way,
than be worried about hell & damnation?

Of course, knowing you as I do,
I'm sure you're headed in the other direction.
And, since you're not in a hurry to get there,
I've canceled your ticket for the next connection.

I've filled this up with love
and wrapped it for safe keeping.
Oh, and when you go to bed tonight,
it damn well better be for sleeping.

............Or whatever!
Love ya *Mom*.

C E L E B R A T E
        THEN
S L E E P   L A T E

HAPPY BIRTHDAY MOM *2006*

Happy Birthday to you *Mom*.
Know where you were last year?
You were at the Libra party,
which means that you were here.

This year I guess you'll miss it,
which means that we'll miss you.
But, you'll be in our thoughts
and we'll toast you a time or two.

You should make some special plans,
put on an evening gown.
You and Cal and Karen
should go out and do the town.

Maybe you and Karen
could rent a room somewhere.
Party at the lounge,
then spend the night right there.

Or, you could visit the Indians
at their reservation.
Play the one armed bandits,
contribute to their *starvation*.

At the very least,
you two should go out to dinner.
Even if you don't come away
from the reservation as a winner.

I've talked with Karen some
and I think we've hatched a plan.
You should celebrate your birthday
the best way that you can.

We all love you *Mom*.
We all wish that you were here.
Guess we'll have to plan better,
when this time comes next year.

Hope you have a special day
and really live it up.
Hope you'll have some *special brew*
inside your coffee cup.

Well here we go again,
it didn't take very long.
Seems every time I turn around
another year has come and gone.

Already it's October and
your birthday's getting near.
When I turn around again
we'll be in another year.

We all wish you well
on this, your special day.
A very Happy Birthday
is what we all wish to say.

I really enjoyed my recent visit,
much of the thanks I owe to you,
but of course, your wonderful daughter
deserves a thank you too.

I enjoyed playing *Gin Rummy*,
even though you kicked my ass,
but the least that I could do,
was lose with a little class.

I even enjoyed playing *Wizard*
and yes, you won that too.
I just didn't want Cal to win
I'd so much rather it be you.

But, the game I enjoyed the most
was the poker that we played.
Yes, you kept on winning,
I should have folded when I stayed.

And, when the session was over
and your money jar over flowed,
you had *Cal* talking to himself
and next day he was on the road.

It did my old heart good
to see him lose for once.
Of all the games we've ever played
he's always won a bunch.

Well, I guess it's time again
for my annual *conditions* report.
There really isn't much news,
so I'll make it kinda short.

The biggest news, I guess,
is that Kevin finally got a job.
They were getting so damn desperate
he was looking for a place to rob.

Just kidding, of course,
but you know what I mean.
Desperate measures are called for
when times get that lean.

Shelly and the girls
seem to be doing just fine.
They've both been getting A's
seems like all the time.

Tim's upholstery work
has picked up a little lately,
but, he's afraid of losing his home,
so he's not living very stately.

He's got a buddy living with him,
waiting for a big settlement to arrive.
He's promised to help him out
so maybe he'll still survive.

Don't see much of Christy,
but she recently turned 16.
She's now at that certain age,
I think you know what I mean.

As for me, I've been quite happy
with the events of the year just passed.
I've been getting out much more
with a lady with lots of class.

She makes me really happy
and we both laugh a lot.
With laughter back in my life,
I'm pleased with what I've got.

I wish there were more to say,
that I had more good news to report,
but I told you in the beginning
I was going to keep it short.

Hope you have a happy birthday
and the family all gets together.
That you get good and *snockered*,
but don't wake *feeling under the weather*.

Love you *Mom*.

MOM'S TEETH

I was cleaning my teeth
and washing my face.
Towels and wash cloths,
all over the place.

I was all lathered up,
getting ready to rinse,
when the water stopped running,
which hasn't happened since.

I should be blonde
and have big tits.
Cause, what I did next
is as dumb as it gets.

I reached over and flushed,
hoping to start water flowing,
made a big mistake,
without even knowing.

As I dried my face
and reached for my teeth,
they were nowhere to be found,
not above or beneath.

It was then that I realized,
flushing was wrong
and as for my teeth,
I just knew they were gone.

I decided to have breakfast,
it was cold cereal day.
Thought I'd let it soak for a while,
then just gum away.

Well, with my very first bite,
I knew something was wrong,
I could tell from the crunch,,,,
my teeth were where they belong.

But, the biggest mistake,
the one I'll never live down,
was telling my daughter,
now it's all over town.

MOM'S 25th ANNIVERSARY *June 8, 1998*

I said it once before,
but I'd like to say it again.
A *mom* is someone special,
that's what you've always been.

You've had this wonderful man
for all these 25 years.
With a guy like him around,
you hadn't many fears.

He was you're knight in shining armor,
your beacon in the night.
He made your days more bearable,
your future seemed more bright.

But, let it not be said,
those things all came for free.
Sometimes he needed looking after.
I'm sure you would agree.

All the demands upon your time,
you've handled with such grace.
Sometimes his wants and needs,
have taken second place.

As a *mother* and a *grandma*,
you've always shined so bright.
But, this man has been there needing,
each and every night.

Let's not forget your needs,
which always seem to come last.
Don't you think it's time,
you put all that in the past?

I've said it all before,
but it should be said again.
It's time you both took first place,
it should be your newest plan.

A twenty five year occasion
should be handled with a trip.
I'd like to contribute to that cause
and don't you give me any lip.

The two of you should try to find
someplace to be alone.
Someplace where you can fish,
or just play bury the bone.

Just wanted to wish you
a happy Thanksgiving.
Heard you had a foot of snow.
Do you really call that living???

You know, it's still not too late
to come down & stay a spell.
You could avoid all that winter
that makes your life a living hell.

I have a spare room
with dressers and all.
No stairs to climb,
so not far to fall.

Course, I really don't know
what Karen would do
if she couldn't spend her evenings
sharing happy hour with you.

But, maybe if you came down
she'd have a reason
to make another trip
and break up the winter season.

I'm enclosing a photo
from Great Granddaughter Christy.
she's such a nice young lady
she makes my eyes get misty.

She's promised me another
for her aunt Karen
as soon as she figures out
what she has left, after sharing.

I'll be talking to you Thursday
about those damn *Detroit Lions*.
They're very disappointing,
but they still keep on trying.

CHAPTER SEVEN
SYMPATHETIC WORDS

Over the years, in addition to my wife, I've lost several really close friends. This chapter attempts to express the sympathy that you feel for their loved ones during those first hurtful days and weeks immediately following that loss. The poem *MY FRIEND LORA* was shared with him just a month or two before his passing.

GOOD BYE BILLY

When a friend I did need,
you were there with great speed.
Whenever I called, you came.

The words weren't profound,
mostly we just hung around,
often we just shot a game.

There wasn't much you could do,
but if it hadn't been for you,
likely I'd have just gone insane.

On the treasure coast,
you'll be missed by a host,
but I'll miss you the most, my friend.

You gave up your fight,
but if your sister is right,
death isn't really the end.

I know you believed,
and I should feel relieved,
to know that you're out of your pain.

Still, it hurts to know
that you had to go,
but someday, I'll see you again.

GOOD BYE FRIEND

Recently our friend began a new journey,
but he'll not make the trip alone.
With him go the best wishes
of everyone he's ever known.

To most he was a friend,
a foe to very few.
Seemed, he a good word
for everyone he ever knew.

Here on the Treasure Coast
he'll be sadly missed.
Those of us at his memorial service,
are but a small portion of the list.

He made a courageous effort,
fought long and hard.
But, it seems that his survival
just wasn't in the cards.

Still, those of us who knew him
have to feel that we were blessed.
Cause, as a father, or a friend,
he was among the very best.

FOR LORA

He was a man who gave much
to the town that he called home.
Though, on that honor roll
he doesn't stand alone.

The list is rather long,
but you'll find him near the top.
When there's trouble who do you call,
a fireman, or maybe a cop?

He left us just a few days ago,
a man I called my friend.
But, according to his daughter
he's yet to reach his journey's end.

He left with many blessings,
yet many blessings did he leave.
She say's I'll see him again,
if I can only learn to believe.

He never waited until you called.
He was always there when needed.
If becoming an angel was his goal,
then I'm convinced that he succeeded.

MY FRIEND LORA

We were *Jaycee's,*
seems like a hundred years ago.
We became pretty good friends,
but just why, I really didn't know.

Seemed we just *hit it off*
and over the years to come,
if I didn't do it with Lora,
seemed it lacked a lot of the fun.

We were *ambulance attenda*nts
and he was a *fireman volunteer.*
Later he became the *Chief,*
elected by his peers.

And when my barn burned,
he was *Johnny on the spot.*
A burned up buggy I had stored,
was all the thanks he got.

In the beginning, we snowmobiled
on a trip he called the stag run.
Sometimes we didn't ride much,
but always, we had fun.

When our boys were playing football
we went to their games together.
With that pouch around his neck,
we fought off lots of nasty weather.

The Second week of Deer Camp
was likely written with him & me in mind.
We never ventured far from camp,
so we'd never be hard to find.

We got into dune buggies
when that became the fad.
And those trips we took to Harrison?
Some of the best I've ever had.

We bowled and golfed together
and sometimes made a friendly bet.
And all my memories of him
are of times I'll never forget.

Later, we played some golf
with a buddy by the name Barrett.
We made a pretty good team,
played any team who'd dare it.

We played pool and pin ball
and sometimes made a friendly wager.
Once we even had a little squabble,
but it was nothing very major.

We also played some cribbage,
a game that was one of his strengths.
He'd always kick my butt,
then we'd share a few more drinks.

We were together through his divorce
and again when my wife died.
When you're facing troubled times
you need a good friend by your side.

I left town years ago
and our friendship suffered some.
But, always when I'd return,
we'd get together for a little fun.

Maybe drinks at the Legion
or possibly a round of golf.
But, we've both mellowed a lot
since I up and headed south.

As he nears the end of his journey
and he faces that final test,
the citizens of Leslie should know
their losing one of their very best.

I think of *Fire Chief Schmit*
and all the time he gave.
The fire department he fought for,
the lives he may have saved.

Then there was *Mr. Dershem*,
who always had my respect.
And, finally *Mr. Miner*,
a hero I didn't expect.

But the hall of fame for Leslie
will never be complete,
if when they call the roll,
Fire Chief Wilson has no seat.

TO CAROLYN

I think I know
what you're going through.
That's why I've been so hesitant
to talk to you.

I know that it feels
like you're going insane,
but I don't know any words
that will ease your pain.

Friends we need,
or we couldn't get by.
But, for those first few weeks
you want only to cry.

Somehow, you get through it,
time moves along.
Suddenly you realize
you're pretty damn strong.

There is life after death
in more ways than one.
There will eventually come a time,
when again you'll have some fun.

You'll never forget him
and just as the hurt starts to fade,
you'll run smack dab into memory,
that the two of you made.

Even after 13 years
there are still occasional tears.
You'll wish you two had shared
just a few more happy years.

But, it wasn't to be.
It wasn't part of the plan.
So, you figure to get by
the best way that you can.

Then one day you realize
that life has been pretty good.
Oh! You'd change a few things,
if there was a way that you could.

But, all things considered
we've been luckier than most
and when we want to reflect,
we each have our own coast.

TROUBLED WATERS FOR MOM

We know life didn't deal you
a hand full of aces.
You've had your share of bad cards
and those without faces.

And now the dealer
has dealt you again.
Will you ever be a winner?
And if so, , , , , when?

We know how difficult
your last months have been.
But, trust me when I say,
there will be laughter again.

And when that time comes,
you will take it in stride.
Knowing some of your feelings
will stay hidden inside.

You'll see a movie,
maybe just hear a song.
It will come flooding back,
is he really gone?

But the memories you have,
of the times that were so dear,
will help you to feel
that he's still very near.

You'll talk to him some,
remember things that he said.
He'll always be with you,
in your heart and your head.

You've always been there,
when there was a need.
When the wrong path was taken
cause' your words we didn't heed.

And, somehow it seems,
we've all muddled through.
Now there are three generations,
all looking up to you.

And, the influence you've had
on how they'll live their lives,
just can't be measured,
even by someone so wise.

You've done your job well.
Done more than your share.
It's time that you knew
just how much we care.

And Maybe, just maybe, , ,
you should swallowed some pride.
Let us carry the load,
just jump on and ride.

GRANDPA WAYNE

My boys and I were talking,
your name came up a lot.
We've heard about your troubles,
and the chances that you've got.

They said, you know that he's our *Grandpa*,
he's the only one we've got.
And, he's always been there for us,
since he and Granny tied the knot.

He was there when I rolled the *Evenrude*,
in fact, he winched me out.
And, when I was learning to shoot my bow,
he showed me what it was all about.

He even gave me my first bow,
then helped me learn to shoot.
Another time, he gave me a shotgun,
he's a generous old coot.

He helped me fix my Bronco
and the things I learned from him,
I've used on other vehicles,
time & time again.

He had a wrench for everything,
sometimes I wondered where they'd been.
He never had a big garage,
to store his tools in.

But, in his little shed,
everything had a place.
I wondered how he could get all those tools,
in that little bitty space.

Whenever anything happened,
he was always Johnny on the spot.
He never seemed judgmental
about all the trouble, into which we got.

He never criticized or condemned,
always seemed to understand.
He always had a hand to lend,
when things didn't go the way we planned,

Now they say your numbers up,
that it's time to pay the piper,
We say, you've beat the odds before,
you just need to remain a fighter.

But if you decide to *hang em up*,
not stick around and fight.
We'd really like for you to know,
we think you've done alright!

CHAPTER EIGHT
CELEBRATIONS

This chapter is about the celebration of life. It's about my wonderful family and the celebration of the many special occasions in life, such as Christmas, birthdays, graduations and milestone anniversary's. It also discusses a special trip to the Florida Keys with my two youngest granddaughters.

CHRISTMAS 1998

Christmas is a special time,
it's my favorite time of year.
It's a time when most of us think of
Santa and all his reindeer.

His elves, toys, and a small pine tree
with lots of decorations.
How in the world will this little fat guy,
make all his destinations?

We think of missile toe,
being on the go.
Frosty and Rudolph,
and having Christmas snow.

Peanut butter fudge, pop corn,
mixed nuts and hard rock candy.
Fruit cake, turkey and dressing,
wouldn't that be dandy?

Pretty lights and packages,
and lots of red and green.
I guess when it comes to Christmas,
we all have our favorite scene.

Maybe it's baby Jesus,
in that manger from afar.
Bethlehem, Joseph & Mary,
or a brightly shining star.

The three wise men, the shepherd,
or maybe just his sheep.
On Christmas eve we need these thoughts
to help us off to sleep.

When we awake on Christmas day,
and find that Santa has been here,
Lord, it's just such a special time,
what a way to end the year.

CHRISTMAS AT KEVIN'S

Well, it's finally Christmas
in the year two thousand & three.
Kylie and Rachel will sing Christmas carols
to Mommy, Daddy and me.

They're pretty little girls,
with beautiful little voices,
singing wonderful songs
and they're all my favorite choices.

After the singing,
we'll all go outside
and with only two wheels,
Kylie will show us she can ride.

And as she rides, close behind
will be her little sister.
Once they'll nearly crash,
but luckily she'll miss her.

When the timing is right,
if I'm not wrong,
Rachel will learn too
and it won't take very long.

Skate boards and roller blades
are surely on the horizon.
Which one, do you think,
will be the first that tries 'em?

They're growing up so fast,
the next thing that you know,
there will be some young man,
wanting them to go see a show.

Then, Mommy and Daddy
will both be singing the blues,
but it won't be the same tune
dear old Grampy would choose.

CHRISTY'S CHRISTMAS, *1998*

It's Christmas time again,
that special time of year,
when everyone wishes
all their friends that special cheer.

When Santa comes to your house,
on this Christmas eve,
with all those wonderful presents
that he'll be planning to leave,,,,

we hope that he'll remember
all the good things you have done.
All the time you've spent with *Grampy,*
cause you're his special one.

We hope your gifts are plenty
and they answer all your needs.
Cause, Santa is a good guy
and he knows of your good deeds.

But, most of all we hope
you'll take this special time,
to think of all the good folks,
who are friends of yours and mine.

There's Kevin, Shelly and Kylie,
Kathy, Mike, BJ & Chad.
Then there's Debbie, Kevin & Matt
MomMom, PopPop, Mommy & Dad.

As this Christmas season passes,
it would mean so very much,
if all these special people
could feel your special touch.

CHRISTY'S GRADUATION, 5th grade 2005

You're leaving elementary,
moving to the big school now.
Just want you to know I'm happy for you
and think you should take a bow.

I heard you made the honor roll,
you've made old Grampy proud.
That's the kind of accomplishment
we should talk about out loud.

One of the worst things you can do
is to waste your time in class.
You've got to be there anyway,
so do twice what you need to pass.

The smartest one has all the *"luck"*
and they usually make more money.
They command the nicest jobs
and the nicest guy's call them *"honey."*

Education is your secret to success.
The crème always rises to the top.
And, let me tell you girl,
you're the *crème of the crop*.

TURNING THIRTEEN - CHRISTY

You're turning thirteen,
a teenager at long last.
You've probably thought of it often
as the years have trickled past.

In a few years you'll be driving,
then out chasing around.
You'll have your own *wheels*
when you go out on the town.

Next, comes graduation.
Hopefully, then on to college.
You should study really hard
gaining a wealth of knowledge.

It's always the smartest people,
who earn the biggest bucks,
but usually the people who *get there*,
don't *get there* just by luck.

You must plan for the results,
someday hopefully you'll be getting.
So, right now is the time
you should do some goal setting.

But, you can't just think them,
they need to be written down.
And, it's not bad to share them
when you have your friends around.

You're known by the company you keep,
as I once told your dad.
Make friends with good people,
try to shy away from the bad.

We'll be family for life,
but your friends will come and go.
So, be selective of the friends
that you really get to know.

You should choose them wisely,
they should have similar goals.
You might be friends forever,
you just never know.

Your goals will keep on changing,
as you attain some and add more.
You must keep adding to the list,
so life won't become a bore.

Plan where you want to be
in five years, or even ten.
Put it on your list,
live your life with a *plan*.

What you get out of life
depends on the goals you spell out.
If it's not heading where you want,
somehow you must turn it about.

Once you've defined a goal,
make plans to attain it.
If you don't put forth some effort,
likely you will never gain it.

Ask questions of yourself.
Is it within my grasp?
What do I need to get there?
Should I take another class?

Constantly, you should be adding
more new goals to your list.
And, read it over often,
are there some you may have missed?

I'm here to tell you girl,
when your life runs out of goals,
you'll feel completely aimless,
like so many other lost souls.

And another thing I'd like to add,
you should try to be more involved.
Extra curricular activities have a purpose
that's the reason they've evolved.

Competition is very healthy
and it teaches many lessons.
Lots of things that you can't get
from academic sessions.

And, I'd recommend choosing
something that will last.
Something that could be a hobby
until your active years have passed.

I'd recommend that you play golf,
of course, it can be expensive,
but you can do it by yourself
until you're not so apprehensive.

Thirteen is a SPECIAL birthday.
But, of course, there will be more.
Each one hopefully more special,
than all the ones before.

Just be sure to enjoy their coming,
cause they come and go real fast.
Try to enjoy every single one
more than you enjoyed the last.

One of life's great secrets
is to always have lots of fun.
Enjoying lots & lots of birthdays
is the best way to get that done.

CELEBRATION

We've traveled separate roads,
now we celebrate our arrival.
The accomplishment of which,
rewards us for our survival.

Life hasn't always been easy,
there's been a bump or two.
But, I'm thankful for my rewards
and especially for you.

HAPPY BIRTHDAY - KAREN

Heard you're having a birthday,
double nickels, so it seems.
Sorry I can't share it with you,
but I'll be there in my dreams.

If there were a magic Genie,
who could make my wish come true,
I'd wish with all my might
to spend that day with you.

Heard you were going to Mt. Pleasant.
To gamble some, I'd guess.
Hope you take lots of cash,
cause you'll likely return with less.

But, when the day is over,
as you're slipping of to sleep,
I hope there'll be more great memories
in the mental scrap book that you keep.

HAPPY BIRTHDAY SIS

A Happy Birthday poem
for my big sister Dee.
One of my favorite people,
if you're not counting me.

She's been through a lot
over these sixty some years.
A lot of great joy,
with a few occasional tears.

She and her man Jack
have shared more than most.
But, they're both a long, long way
from giving up the ghost.

And, there's three generations
looking up to them now,
making four generations
looking over their *bow*.

So, they scuttled the ship
and bought a house on wheels.
It's a place to sleep
and share most of their meals.

Cause, they travel a lot,
at least that's how it seems.
And, they've more traveling to do
to fulfill all their dreams.

It's now getting close
to the time when they will go.
Where do you think they're heading?
Which way does the wind blow?

You see, they are sailors at heart
and the wind has been their guide.
And, there are many other things,
that still they haven't tried.

So, we're having a party,
sending them off on their way.
Unless we can convince them
that they might better stay.

KYLIE, One year old

Grampy loves you,
oh yes he does.
You're one of the sweetest
that there ever was.

Mommies love their babies,
daddy's love them too,
but not the same way
that Grampys always do.

You're only one,
and already we see,
the elegant lady,
someday you'll be.

Today there's just one candle,
in the middle of your cake.
You're so young and tender,
so many mistakes yet to make.

One day you'll smile
and hearts will break.
Then one fine day
there's a groom on your cake.

First thing you know,
your parents are grand.
Next thing you know,
they're covered with sand.

Life goes by us,
so gol darn fast,
one day you're old
and it's all in the past.

Live it to the fullest,
don't waste a moment.
If you see something you want,
make plans to own it.

When it's all said and done
and you're as old as me,
your thoughts should be pure
and your heart should be free.

HAPPY BIRTHDAY KYLIE, August 4, 2006

If I'm not mistaken,
This year you're turning nine.
You're growing up so fast
and growing up so fine.

So, you're going to Orlando
with your sister, Mom & Dad.
Hope you enjoy your trip.
Hope it's the best you've ever had.

Heard about your singing,
that you made your parents proud.
If I'd have been there to see it.
I'd have clapped really, really loud.

Everybody told me
what a really good job you did.
They said when you finished,
you ducked your head and hid.

Wish I'd have been there to watch,
but I hear there's hope for me.
Seems, your mom has it on video
and she promised to let me see.

For now, enjoy your birthday
and enjoy the weekend too.
When you get back, I want pictures
of all the things you see & do.

KYLIE IN THE KEYS

Today's the day that Kylie & Mom
go swimming with the dolphins.
In a few more years these same two
will likely spend their spare time golfin'.

She's been so looking forward,
to this adventure by the sea.
Yesterday was her sister's turn
and she watched with Dad and me.

Finally! The day has come,
but we can't seem to find the place.
I think she's really getting worried,
by the look upon her face.

She doesn't want to miss it,
but time is running out.
We stopped and asked directions,
then turned the car about.

At last, we finally find the place
and the trainer gave us her talk.
Then, we take a boat ride
after we go out this wooden walk.

Mom goes first and Kylie is second,
so she had to wait her turn.
She watched every thing Mom did
to see what she could learn.

Now she's in the water,
with a dolphin on each side.
Then she holds out her arms
and they take her for a ride.

She gets to hug a dolphin.
From another she gets a kiss.
Of all the fun things on our trip,
nothing compares to this.

She then lays on her back,
with the dolphins at her feet.
They push her around backwards
and she thinks its really neat.

She and Mom hold up a hoop
for the dolphins to jump through.
This is only one of the tricks,
that these beautiful mammals do.

Today was her special day.
Would she forget it? NEVER!
She says, "thank you Mom & Dad,
I'll remember this forever."

RACHEL IN THE KEYS

Today's the day that Rachel & Mom
go swimming with the sea lions.
Mom worries that she'll be afraid
and hopes she don't start cryin'.

But, she seems to be so brave
and with her face all aglow,
she's at the front of the line.
She's ready and rarin' to go.

She swims the length of the pond
with a lion swimming by her side.
They seem so close and friendly,
you wish you could get on and ride.

They all do some tricks,
one even gives her a hug and a kiss.
And every time they do it right,
the trainer gives them a fish.

They tell her about a newborn,
but it's too young to come out to play.
They keep it in a special pen
to keep the kids away.

She got to talk to the bird lady
and watch the dolphin show.
She wishes she could stay
but she knows it's time to go.

As the saying goes, "all good things
must come to an end."
but think of all the stories
she can now tell to all her friends.

Today is her favorite part of the trip
so many sights to see.
She says, "Thank you Mom and Dad,
for this special day you gave to me."

145

RACHEL'S BIRTHDAY

Today you're turning 3years old,
it's your special day.
You're growing up so fast,
in every single way.

I remember when you'd cry
every time you saw me.
But, that was long before
the day that you turned three.

Someday soon
you'll be going to school.
Next thing you know,
you'll make some boy your fool.

In a short time you'll be driving,
then going to college,
spending dad's bucks,
gaining great knowledge.

Somewhere along the way
you'll probably bend a rule.
But, nothing will stop you
from graduate school.

Then one day,
you'll meet that special guy.
He'll be the one
who puts a twinkle in your eye.

On the day of your marriage,
you'll think it's the best.
But, please don't forget
about all of the rest.

So many milestones,
coming your way.
But, none more special,
than this very day.

MY GRANDDAUGHTER RACHEL

She's such a pretty young lady,
the young men will someday swoon.
She's my granddaughter Rachel
and her birthday is coming soon.

If three can be known as such,
she's the baby of the *bunch.*
But, she's wise beyond her years,
at least that would be my hunch.

She seems to be a great student,
she's been getting lots of A's.
We hope she keeps on studying
and that's the way it always stays.

She follows Mom's example
I guess it's *just because.*
So, I expect great success for her,
a leader in all she does.

She's been a very good cheerleader
for quite some time now.
She's doing really great
and she really should take a bow.

She's always been athletic,
from Grampy's point of view,
always learning to do things
all the older girls would do.

She's always been so loving,
always the first to tell me hi.
And, when it's time to leave,
she always gives me a hug goodbye.

Grampys don't play favorites,
or so people have said to me,
but if I had to choose a favorite,
she's definitely in my top three.

147

MY DAUGHTER-IN-LAW, SHELLY

Our branch of the King family
was the smallest of the tree.
But, our branch began to grow
when Kevin married Shelly.

First they bought a house in Louisville,
it was their brand new digs.
Then our branch of the tree
sprouted two more twigs.

They had two little baby girls
and before they even started school,
they decided to move to Florida,
cause they were nobody's fool.

So their house went on the market,
sold in just a few short weeks.
They even made a small profit
much like everybody seeks.

Then they bought a house in Florida
located near a great big park.
Now they have lots of cats,
but their dog, *Izzy*, no longer barks.

They're happy, so it seems
and so are those little babies.
Well, they're not babies anymore,
they've turned into little ladies.

They're being brought up proper,
being allowed to spread their wings.
One's a burgeoning cheerleader
and the other acts and sings.

Their mom is exposing them to choices,
things like soccer, music and dance.
You'll never know where their talents lead
if you don't give different things a chance.

She's a really talented lady,
of whom I'm really proud.
I think the world of her,
she'd stand out in any crowd.

She's a pretty special person
and she's motivated to succeed.
Has she improved our family bloodline?
I'd say she has indeed.

HAPPY BIRTHDAY MARILYN

I wanted to write you a birthday poem,
but I wasn't sure just what to say.
Should I be serious?
Well, as you know, that's just not my way.

Should I be tender and loving?
No, that time for us has passed.
I could try a little humor,
but I just can't think that fast.

So, I decided to be truthful.
You might not expect that from me.
Although, in all of our past dealings,
that's what I've always tried to be.

It's a Happy Birthday poem
for one of my dearest friends.
One of my favorite people,
not yet wearing *depends*.

You've been through a lot
over these sixty plus years.
A lot of great joys
and more than the occasional tear.

But, you've handled it very well,
or at least that's what I've been told.
They say, *At least she has,*
for someone who's grown so old.

You're really a wonderful person
with an extremely wonderful soul,
even though all of those years
have taken quite a toll.

I'd like to welcome you to *AARP*
and your first Social Security check.
We're not so young anymore,
but it's free money so what the heck.

Well, I guess it's really not free,
we've all paid a price,
but the fact we have it coming
makes living twice as nice.

WAYNE'S 25th ANNIVERSARY *(6/8/98)*

For one man's image,
in his sweetie's eyes to shine.
Twenty Five years
is a long damn time.

After all those years,
at least once or twice,
there must have been times,
you thought she wasn't so nice.

But, you toughed it out,
fought through the pain
and you've made 25 years
without going insane.

I know there were times
when you two didn't agree.
Times when she said two,
and you wanted three.

That's when you negotiate,
or just stop talking.
With a lot of couples,
one party talks about *walking*.

She's a hell of a woman
she deserves a lot.
You've given your all,
everything that you've got.

Although she's a great lady,
she does have her *ways*.
And you've earned my respect
for how you handled those days.

152

We don't call you dad,
but not because we don't care,
believe me when I tell you,
we were so glad you were there.

They say the *Golden Years*
are sometimes filled with rust.
We'd all like to spend those years,
with someone we can trust.

She's as lucky to have you,
as you are to have her.
Now spend the rest of your lives,
just making sure.

40 YEARS TOGETHER – Bill & Carol

In olden days,
when Billy was young,
why you just wouldn't believe,
some of the things he's done.

Now he's a little older
and he may have slowed a bit
but still he finds it hard
to do nothing, but just sit.

Now that he's retired,
he doesn't work as hard.
Yet, he still finds time
to take care of his own yard.

Yup, the fire's still there
and of course the brain still works,
only now he doesn't have to deal
with quite so many jerks.

The TV and newspaper
get more of his attention
and he wouldn't miss CNN,
that really needs to be mentioned.

And of course he's got the cottage
that sits beside the river.
Seems there's always something to do,
or some thing he needs to deliver.

You wonder how he finds the time
to winter at the Holiday Out.
It just seems that he enjoys his life
and that's what it's all about.

And Carol, what a lady!
And, what a gracious host.
Bet she's the Grandma,
that her grandkids want to visit most.

She always makes you feel at home
always has kind words.
She makes you feel like number one,
never second or third.

Now they've come upon 40 years,
some with storms they've had to weather.
But, mostly it's been 40 years
of blissful life together.

50 YEARS TOGETHER – Tom & Jean

Fifty years as man and wife
makes for a very special occasion.
Course, you have to be fairly old
to be found in that situation.

Lots of water under the bridge
and lots of ground you've covered.
Lots of beautiful memories
and a few needing to be smothered.

You've raised a wonderful family,
now into it's 4th generation.
All that time you've stayed the course
to accomplish this celebration.

We're not promised easy,
nor are we promised time.
We're not even promised the friendship
that you two were able to find.

I'm sure you'd make minor changes
were you given that chance.
But, from where I sit the two of you
have most enjoyed life's dance.

When all is said and done,
there's really only one true test.
Would you do it all again?
I believe you'd both say yes!

GLEN & JANE - 50 YEARS TOGETHER

In days of old, when Glen was young,
you wouldn't believe some of the things he's done.
Now that he's older, he's slowed a bit
and sometimes now, all he does is sit.

Oh, the fire is there and the brain still works,
but now he don't have to deal with all the jerks.
The TV and newspaper get more of his attention
and one other thing, we probably shouldn't mention.

He hardly works, though he used to work hard,
yet he still found time to take care of his yard.
And, when I used to visit with those kids of mine,
he always found time to go wet a line.

When Kevin and Timbo each caught their first fish,
East Lake was the place, we still remember this.
Uncle Glen wasn't there the day of the event,
but we all were, because of the cabin he'd lent.

Aunt Jane, what a lady, a most gracious host.
The aunt that we all wanted to visit the most.
She made us and our kids all feel right at home.
I still think of those times, as I sit here alone.

When our mom died, if I could choose another,
she'd have been the one I'd have chosen for my mother.
We didn't see her much, though it wasn't that far,
a couple times each year, we'd all jump in the car.

The door was always open, no matter what time of year,
she made room for us all and our snowmobile gear.
For a funeral or wedding or a special get together,
she'd take us all in and to hell with the weather.

I miss those times, now that I've moved south,
but those kinds of words seldom come from my mouth.
They're in my heart and often on my mind,
but the proper words are just so hard to find.

I wish I could be there for your special day,
but my son, Kevin, and his wife are coming to stay.
Lakeland will be calling and as that time draws near,
you can be sure I won't miss it, again this year.

50th ANNIVERSARY - FOR AUNT JANE

He was my warrior, my shining knight.
He made my future seem so very bright.
Like most men, he had some flaws,
but not enough to make me pause.

He comforted me, when he had the time,
when he wasn't out trying to make a dime.
Seemed there was always another job,
Peter or Paul, which one should we rob.

Times weren't bad, though we complained,
seemed like it poured, whenever it rained.
We scrimped and saved to buy a home,
Just a little place where we could be alone.

They say it's darkest, before the dawn,
but it sure got brighter when the twins came along.
A little girl and her little brother,
we said to ourselves, can we afford another?

In those days, we weren't all that smart
and we sometimes got the horse, before the cart.
As you might guess, there came a day,
when little Marsha came our way.

As time moved on, we prospered some,
though not by the standards of everyone.
We had our setbacks, but don't we all?
Somehow we managed, to answer the call.

One day we noticed, the children were grown.
The girls were gone, we got back our phone.
Life begins at 40, so they say,
But my man & I , we say no way.

Our lives began when we first met.
and we both know, it's not over yet.
We may be older, we may have slowed,
but we still have some oats needing to be sowed.

50th ANNIVERSARY - FOR UNCLE GLEN

Fifty years is a long damn time,
to spend with any woman, other than mine.
She's made me happy, all of the way,
so very happy, still does today.

There was a time I didn't know
what to do, or which way to go.
She was my beacon in those days,
she cast the light and showed me the way.

We've had our tough times, as most people have.
She always healed me, she was my salve.
She always knew what I needed most,
and when people visited, she was the host.

She kept me going when times got tough,
she always knew, when I'd had enough.
She bore my children, she made me proud,
she cooled me down, when I got loud.

When there were times that I took a drink,
she always made me stop and think.
She knew her man had a few little flaws,
but she never let me give up the cause.

All those reunions at the lake,
all those things she had to bake.
She never complained or made a fuss,
she always said, "Come back and see us."

She made me happy, I'm sure she knows,
though I seldom took time, to give her a rose.
Together, we've shared a million tears,
now we've come upon fifty years.

She stuck with me through thick & thin.
So many times, she was there again.
She was my beacon, still is today,
I wouldn't want it any other way.

Fifty years ain't near enough time,
for me to spend with this gal of mine.
We may have to ask for help from above,
but we need more time to use up our love.

AUNT JANE NINETY?

I've heard your having a birthday,
a milestone not many have seen.
Bet you never thought about this day,
back there in your teens.

Course, our minds seldom travel
that far ahead in time.
And, in our teens other things
seemed to occupy our mind.

You've traveled life's many roads,
experienced a bump or two, so it seems.
You've learned most all of life's lessons,
lived most all your dreams.

As you look back on life,
with more yesterdays than tomorrows,
count up all the blessings,
don't dwell on any sorrows.

Several generations
are now looking up to you.
And, the lessons you have taught
show in all they say and do.

So enjoy your special day,
knowing you have done your part
and though many of us won't be there,
you're still within our heart.

It's a day for celebration,
a day to congregate.
A day to eat your birthday cake
with no worries about gaining weight.

CHAPTER 9
PURSUIT OF TOMORROW

During the search for my tomorrow there have been a number of missteps, but often times a path in the wrong direction can reveal many truths. Life is an adventure and frequently we profit from our mistakes. One of my fondest memories from my days of deer hunting involved a huge buck, which I spotted during the one and only time that I was fool enough to venture alone far enough from camp to get lost. And so it was during the search for my dream girl. Although she was difficult to find, it wasn't always wasted time. I'm whom I am today because of the acquaintances I've made along the way.

YOU CAN'T GO BACK

Right or left, which should I choose?
Or, does it really matter?
I chose the fore, but if that was wrong,
should I have chosen the latter?

She wanted me to love her.
She wanted to be my wife.
Love her I almost did,
but still, I had to live my life.

Now, as I look back,
we shared the best of times.
Oh, it wasn't always perfect,
but it was mostly pretty fine.

I know the decision I made
may have turned out wrong.
It's one of life's many lessons,
and I'd known that all along.

It seemed we had it going,
that we were really on our way,
but a fork came in our road
and somehow we went astray.

Life is full of twists and turns,
it's about making many choices.
And, if the choice you make is wrong,
you'll be hearing little voices.

If the turn we took was wrong,
we didn't know it at the time.
We both paid a price,
but I just couldn't toe her line.

You can never go back,
it's been so often said.
Still, for months thoughts of her
kept running through my head.

SHE'LL NEVER KNOW

Last night, she called me
on my cellular phone.
She didn't need to ask,
but yes, I was alone.

She said where are you at?
What's been going on?
We'd like to join you,
hang out and have some fun.

She said we're having a few drinks
and reliving old times.
Times, she felt quite certain,
partially were mine.

Later, when they joined me
she had me quite excited.
Seemed there was still a spark,
but somehow it never ignited.

We had several drinks
and talked for a little while
and she favored me some
with her own special smile.

I shook hands with her son
and spoke with a niece I know.
We weren't together very long
before I decided it was time to go.

She'll likely never know
that she nearly owned my heart,
or how I've enriched her life
by the fact we're now apart.

I couldn't make her happy,
nor could she do that for me.
But, at least, by being apart
we now had a chance to be.

She was once special to me
she knew that, I'm quite certain.
But, as far as having a relationship,
we had drawn the final curtain.

WHEN THE LOVIN' JUST UP & ENDS

Once, she was my lover.
Now, we're barely even friends.
It's amazing how you grow apart
when the lovin' just up and ends.

First, we thought it was our time.
Next, we were trying to make amends.
But, it seems much less important
when the lovin' just up and ends.

Oh, once in a while we still talk,
but only now and then.
And, of course, there's no intimacy
once the lovin' just up and ends.

Eventually you move along.
But, just how quickly really depends
on how well you're prepared
for when the lovin' just up and ends.

One day you start to live again,
you'll finally meet a caring friend.
Eventually you'll find yourself hoping
the lovin' never just up and ends.

That future is now my present,
though it took me a while to mend.
For over a year, it's been my hope
that this lovin' never just up and ends.

THEN CAME HALLOWEEN

Sittin' on a stool
at the end of the bar.
When in walked Cleopatra,
looking hot as fire.

She frittered all around,
said all of her hello's,
then the stool beside me
was the one she finally chose.

We'd had a lengthy history,
but that didn't really matter.
She gave me a friendly hug,
then we began to chatter.

There's a new man in her life,
he really seemed quite nice.
But, she and I had been together
more than once or twice.

They were dressed in costume,
he even offered me a smoke.
It was a Marlboro red,
not the kind that you toke.

Later, she and I talked,
after he had stepped away.
But, you can't go back in time,
I think it's safe to say.

She had me against the wall
and I'll admit to a moments desire.
I could have been with her again,
but our time had long ago expired.

I'd always known that it was over,
that was always understood.
She and I together
just didn't work out so good.

There are no second thoughts
about what I really feel.
She almost had me going,
but I knew it wasn't real.

We'd been apart so long
and had very little contact,
now it seemed a possibility,
but I still didn't want her back.

A LOST GEM

Lord knows she wasn't perfect,
but then again, was I?
As long as we didn't dwell on it,
we were able to get by.

Almost from the beginning
we just seemed to click.
I just couldn't believe it.....
What was up with this chick?

With our very first dance,
we just seemed to melt.
Later that same night,
was like nothing I'd recently felt.

We made a few memories,
time slipped by real fast.
Now, it seems so obvious
that our time has long since passed.

Oh, she still enters my thoughts
and at times, I still fantasize.
Even though its been a few years
since we said our last goodbye's.

She was looking for a husband.
I was looking to be a friend.
She wanted either a ring,
or the relationship to end.

She needed a ceremony
if she was to ever feel secure.
I was either too damn stubborn,
or felt just too unsure.

We had our chance,
but it's long since slipped away.
Was that a big mistake?
I really don't see it that way.

Still, at times I wonder,
given one more chance,
if I were to ask again,
do you think that she would *dance*?

Lord knows that we weren't perfect.
It seemed the world could see.
The relationship was flawed,
but she was awfully good to me.

REMINISCENCES

With our very first dance,
we just seemed to melt.
Later that same night,
was like nothing I've ever felt."

In an earlier poem,
I wrote that very verse.
How do those things happen
when we didn't even rehearse?

I wasn't really a smoker,
although I had occasionally smoked.
We went out to her car,
fired one up and we toked…..

Then, the two of us danced
around a tiny, dimly lit floor.
Dirty Dancing you might call it,
each wanting something more.

We just seemed to *fit*.
She knew my every move.
Course, after that *toke*
I just felt I couldn't lose.

And after that night,
seemed we were always together.
It didn't occur to us to ask,
Why? When? or Whether?

We must have discussed
what we thought would be our future,
but I guess we never agreed.
Maybe we just weren't that sure.

Whatever it was,
or was supposed to be,
it's obvious that it wasn't,
or so it seemed to me.

I miss those days,
though I can't say exactly why.
Seemed we had lots of fun.
Still, one day we said goodbye.

We've both moved on.
There's a new man in her life
and I'm much happier knowing
she has no plans to be my wife.

ONE BAD TURN AFTER ANOTHER

Seems I took a wrong turn
when I turned down this lonely road.
I've been seeking my way back,
carrying my load.

I should have turned left,
but instead I turned to the right.
I should have turned around,
given another chance, I might.

She turned off the TV,
turned on the stereo,
tuned in a country station,
turned it down real low.

She turned on the music,
then blew me off my feet.
She had turned my head,
then turned up the heat.

She had turned me on,
then she turned me down.
Finally, when she turned to me,
I just turned around.

We still had a chance
but we couldn't turn the page.
Seems we took a wrong turn
and love turned into rage.

I might have taken a wrong turn.
My life may never turn out the same,
but I've turned over a new leaf
and I'm still in the game.

It's been one bad turn after another,
but it's turning out alright.
I've turned my life around
and this time the turn feels right.

I made all those bad turns,
but that's the way we learn.
She'd had control all along.
Now, finally it's my turn.

CHAPTER 10
THE GIRL FROM MY DREAMS

Over 22 years after my wife passed away and after several unsuccessful attempts to find that perfect person, I accidentally found myself *online* with a computer dating service. "What the heck," I thought, "why not give it a shot?" Its the best decision I've made in recent memory. Some of the poems in this chapter were written with the lady that I met through that service as the subject, *way before I had even met her*. She truly is *the girl from my dreams*. We both feel so blessed that we discovered each other. However, we have always *traveled in different circles*, it's very unlikely that we would have ever crossed paths had it not been for the dating service. I'm convinced that my *PURSUIT* is over.

MY MATCH

They met on the computer.
They'd each spent time alone.
If they really connected,
maybe then they'd try the phone.

Each had lost their spouse,
both had died of cancer.
Each had done some seeking,
neither had found the answer.

In the beginning she had lots of questions.
He had questions too.
They'd ask them of each other,
like all new couples do.

They'd ask them over the internet,
cause she was miles away.
Seemed that made it easier,
face to face he had so little to say.

She was preparing for a family wedding,
for a month would be out of state.
He wondered, could they wait that long,
to be together for that *first date*.

They'd both spent time in Michigan.
They'd both worked in a bank.
He asked if she played golf,
was she familiar with a *shank*?

He wondered if she played pool
and could she handle a cue?
Without his favorite entertainment,
whatever would they do?

She spoke of playing euchre,
since they'd both lived in the North.
He wondered if they'd share a ride
next time they went back and forth.

She asked him what's your favorite beer
and what's your favorite dessert?
How long ago did your wife die?
Do you ever get over the hurt?

They both grew more bold
the questions, more intense.
She asked was he a boob guy?
His answer made no pretense.

He could take or leave the boobs,
though some might think him nuts.
He guessed if he were truthful,
he looked first at really nice butts.

They spoke about their musical tastes
and of the movies they'd enjoyed,
about raising their children
and the places they'd been employed.

Did he like karaoke and
did he sing by any chance?
Had he ever been on a cruise?
Did he like to dance?

Was he a good kisser
and did he enjoy the act?
She was destined to find out,
she knew that for a fact.

He joked that being so sweet,
when it rained, he'd likely melt.
Rain melted salt too,
was the way she said she felt.

179

She wondered how many girl friends
he'd spent his time with
and did he have any love left over,
that he was willing to give?

His answer wasn't exactly
what she was looking for,
but he hadn't given his all
and felt certain he had more.

What would the women from his past
have to say to her?
Was it really over
and did they know that for sure?

Neither could believe
just how bold they had become.
Somehow, talking on the internet
was becoming so much fun.

Life isn't so enjoyable
without someone to share.
Someone who's your everything
and for whom you truly care.

Someone to be your comrade,
yet often so much more.
Your day and night companion,
even though you sometimes snore.

The questions keep on coming,
the answers incomplete,
yet they agree computer dating
is a wonderful way to meet.

QUESTIONS

Is writing poetry to your sweetheart
really that old fashioned?
Even when it's written words,
isn't it still called passion?

Would we ever know true happiness,
if we've never experienced sorrow?
Since the day that we first met
you've been my new tomorrow.

Would we ever enjoy our companionship,
if we'd never been alone?
Could I appreciate your warmth
without the loneliness I've known.

Could we maintain our sanity
without just a little madness?
Can we ever experience real joy,
if we haven't known some sadness?

Would we ever enjoy a rainbow
if there were never any rain?
Could we even recognize pure pleasure,
if we never suffered pain?

Could we recognize true beauty,
without the ugly side of life?
Will we ever know contentment,
without a little stress & strife?

Could we ever be courageous,
if we've never been afraid?
Would we ever feel real trust,
if we've never been betrayed?

Could we really appreciate our freedom,
if we never have felt caged?
Could we ever feel compassion
if we haven't known some rage?

Can we ever experience love,
if we've never known hate?
Can we ever know contentment,
if we've never tempted fate?

Would we appreciate the sunshine,
if there were never a cloudy day?
Would we know about true love,
had we arrived here a different way?

I don't have the answers.
They're just questions, don't you see?
But, we could seek them together,
if you'll just come along with me?

MY NEW FRIEND

I met this real nice lady
just a few months ago.
She makes me want her with me,
wherever I may go.

I really like her attitude,
it matches mine a lot.
She might say, "Forget it, do it tomorrow,
today it's just too hot."

She'll say, "That's why they call it retirement."
Or, "Tomorrow's another day."
And, "We'll get to it, when we have time."
sounds like something she might say.

Nothing seems to *ruffle her feathers*.
She's what I'd call *easy going*.
And, she never has to prove herself,
though always, she's all knowing.

We 'don't *get above our raisin*,'
but I'm satisfied with what we've got.
She's always fun to be around,
although we might not do a lot.

We've lots of things in common,
though that's not what matters most.
It's that comfort that we feel
when either of us plays host.

We've had similar backgrounds,
both having spent some time in banking.
And we've each lost a spouse to cancer,
for which there's no one we'll be thanking.

Yet, when all is said and done,
you make the best of the hand your dealt
and if I had never have met her,
these feelings I'd never have felt.

A CHRISTMAS POEM FOR DONNA

It's the very first Christmas
we'll be spending together.
It seems we're both hoping
it's the 1st of forever.

We're new to each other,
but we've made a great start.
It's a fantastic beginning,
we both feel in our heart.

And likely we'll not be needing
bouquets of mistletoe,
You only need that
when you're kissing for show.

We need not ask….
Permission we do not seek.
We've had *10 second kisses*
since our very first week.

The mission it seems,
for her and for me,
is to spend time together,
yet continue to feel free.

But, as the season approaches
and the day draws near,
we try to calm each other
of our greatest fear.

We've each been alone,
it was a part of our fate,
but alone and loneliness.
need not share the same plate.

Together we've bonded,
we've grown to be friends.
We need to insure that the friendship
never comes to an end.

Though marriage isn't likely,
it's not out of the question.
But, it's more like we're together
for a lifelong *session*.

And during this holiday season
of festive good cheer,
it's our mutual hope
that the other always is near.

A SINGLE MAN I AM

I'm perfectly happy
being completely alone.
There's always peace and quiet
here in my little home.

I do my own cooking,
though its sometimes kinda chancy
and I do my own dirty dishes,
when ever it strikes my fancy.

I do my own house cleaning,
sweep and mop my own floors,
do my own grocery shopping
and carry them through my own door.

I have no guilty feelings,
no apologies to make.
I never ask permission
for the liberties I might take.

I do pretty much as I please,
never having to ask.
I make no explanations,
no one ever takes me to task.

Still, at times it gets lonely,
living life alone.
No one there to help
make my house into a home.

They say that men can't,
(or maybe won't) commit.
The words *I do* are simple,
but they're words I can't permit.

I'm not a fearful man
and I have a kindly heart,
but it scares me so to think,
"Until death do we part"

I've traveled that road
and in fact, she has too.
But, those five words are scary.
The ones preceding the words *I do*

Still, when the nights get lonely
and I'm longing for a friend,
she's the one I think of
time and time again.

Guess, I'm not really all that happy
and likely neither is she.
We'd probably both be much closer,
If *she* and *I* were *we*.

Life might not be perfect,
but it could be much closer than this.
We'd likely enjoy it more
if we shared a daily *10 second kiss*.

That's directly from TV,
Sweetie heard on some show.
Some expert brought it up
and he'd be the one to know.

When we share our world,
waking beside her is divine.
But, just before we fall asleep
is the most fantastic time.

I WANT TO SHARE WITH YOU

I've written a number of poems,
some I've shared with you.
There are others that I've written,
but sharing them, I'm not ready to do.

Often the things I write,
are just for me to see.
Usually they're about certain things
that are very personal to me.

Lately, some of my writings
have included thoughts of you.
I've been experiencing these strange feelings
that, for me at least, are new.

I've never been impulsive,
I've always tried to think things through.
At least that could be said,
until the day I first wrote you.

You've messed with my head.
You've scrambled up my brain.
I've been so long alone,
I'm unfamiliar with the terrain.

For years I've been a bachelor.
That's the life I know.
I'm not used to being with someone
wherever I may go.

You're really very special.
You need only to believe.
I want to share more time with you
and there's nothing up my sleeve.

But, finding someone so special
wasn't something I had planned.
I'm not quite ready to commit
and need to know you understand.

I probably don't deserve you,
but, I'll try hard to earn that right.
And if you'll be very patient,
in time,,,, some day,,,, I might.

Even though I'm still not certain
of the direction we should take,
for the short time we have left,
nothing should be fake.

For me, you're picture perfect.
I'm very comfortable with our fit.
And, I'm pretty sure my comfort
is as good as it can get.

Yet, I still can't promise
never will we part.
I've lived a life of bachelorhood
and it's still within my heart.

But, if some day we should separate,
you can be sure of it.
The reason will never be,
that I found a better fit.

Here and now I promise
always to be true.
Never shall you need to wonder
if there's someone other than you.

TOO YOUNG FOR BINGO

First we met for ice cream,
then I took her for a ride.
We've since done lots of other things
and we're usually side by side.

We're not old enough for *Bingo*,
or so she'd have me think.
And, usually when we go out
she'll only have one drink.

We have a movie night
and we sometimes go to *karaoke*.
So far everything we've done
she says is *okie dokie*.

We may go out dancing,
or maybe just to dinner.
Then I'll have my poker day,
but daily, I'm the winner.

For now, our time together
I treasure in my heart.
And, I think about her often
whenever we're apart.

But, neither of us are thinking
of a 24/7 relationship.
And, we don't say I love you,
unless we let it slip.

I'll just tell her she *smells good*,
she knows it's part of my spiel.
It's from a guy on TV,
maybe from *Boston Legal*.

We both know the other cares
and we're having lots of fun.
Even without the rings & license,
I'm certain she's the one.

So, the last thing every evening
as I'm heading off to bed,
rather than that old loneliness,
I think of her instead.

I CAN HEAR HER MUSIC

The first thing every morning,
she's the first thought in my head.
I'm thinking of things I'll write to her
even before I get out of bed.

Then, as the day progress's,
seems the whole day long,
her image comes to mind
with every other song.

It might be a *Country Classic*,
or any common country tune,
but I can hear her music
from every single room.

It's the same thing every evening,
as I sit and watch TV.
I'm just waiting for the time
when she'll be sitting next to me.

I'm sure it wouldn't be that hard
to see each other more.
But, if we lived in the same zip code
we'd be constantly at each other's door.

Now, we email each other often,
or send an instant message.
Sometimes just a line or two,
sometimes we fill the page.

Usually every evening,
some time shortly after eight,
she'll buzz me on instant message,
and we'll sit & *conversate*.

Oh, I know that's not a word,
but it's the best that I could do.
We *ratchet jaw* about everything
so it's the closest I could choose.

We'll both be watching something
then on comes a commercial.
So, we'll send each other a message,
sort of our personal infomercial.

We'll both get a real good laugh,
or maybe just a giggle,
then go back to the show,
when one of us gives the signal.

Back and forth we'll go,
just talking silly stuff,
though it's generally not important,
seems we never get enough.

The point I'm trying to make,
is with so much time on the internet,
we probably get in lots more words,
than most other couples get.

What we say is not important,
only that we converse
and I still hear her music,
as I work on my next verse.

A DREAM COME TRUE

Their paths crossed,
like a head on collision.
She could be no more perfect,
had she come in a vision.

Had he dreamed her up,
to be precise,
he wouldn't have dreamed her
to be this nice.

To choose a word
and to be real specific.
His word for her
would be terrific.

She is his goal.
She's the air that he breathes.
She resurrected his soul.
She made him believe.

She is his queen.
Yet, he knows not what to do.
She's not a dream,
but a dream come true.

She is his future.
She blurs his past.
She'll be his always.
She'll be his last.

DREAM OR A NIGHTMARE?

In my dream they tell me
you've a short time to live.
To myself, I say,
who will I spend it with?

To me the answer,
wasn't really a surprise.
I'd spend it with that gal
who smiles with her eyes.

Though we've only recently met,
it seems we've made a connection.
We're not there yet,
but we're headed in that direction.

So, when they come to tell me
that the end is drawing near,
my thoughts all dwell on her
and the reason seems so clear.

With time, we'd be happy,
she'd be my very best friend.
We'd share all the good times
until I've rounded that bend.

For the last twenty years
I've gotten by some way.
No real plan for the future,
just living for the day.

Finally, when I find her
they say there's no cure.
So, I set my final goal
to spend eternity with her.

I don't ever want to cause her
a single moment of displeasure,
but I'd sure like to leave her with
some great memories to treasure.

MY DREAM GIRL

I dreamed of her companionship.
I'd been so long alone.
And, the passion she made me feel
was unlike any I'd recently known.

I was so lucky to have her love,
but there was a barrier in our way.
Still, I kept my fingers crossed,
that in time, we'd have our day.

She brought me so much pleasure,
and though we were still apart,
often we were together
deep within my heart.

Someday we'd know contentment,
I was confident of this.
I was longing for her touch,
and to share her passionate kiss.

I was looking for a future
without much time to spare.
It seemed it was our destiny,
there was much we'd yet to share.

It was hard to be without her,
for in my mind, I had atoned.
But, if it was never going to be,
maybe I could have her cloned.

Meantime, I'd write her poems,
although, it did seem a bit old fashioned.
It was a shame she'd never see them,
still,,, my mind had known her passion.

after so much time without her
I had experienced a bit of sorrow.
But now, since Baskin Robbins,
I foresee a bright tomorrow.

Dreams sometimes seem real.
The passion, sometimes intense.
Now, I may have met my dream girl
and these words begin to make more sense.

NO LONGER ALONE

He'd been on his own
for quite a long time.
She started new thoughts
creeping into his mind.

He'd been satisfied with life,
the way things had been.
She started him thinking
about actually living again.

She made him think
about getting out now and then.
About having some fun
enjoying the company of a friend.

He now knew he wanted someone
with whom he could share,
with whom he would enjoy life
and for whom he could care.

He wanted someone who would help him
come up from the past,
create a new future
and do it with class.

Oh, he's set in his ways,
but he thinks he can change,
if the lady he spends time with
doesn't cause him more pain.

Yah, he'd been alone,
and was doing just fine,
but now being alone
didn't seem quite so sublime.

Life's just too damn short
to live it without passion
and with her on his arm
he now feels more *in fashion*.

WHAT IF ?

What if I didn't have you?
Then again, what if I really and truly did?
What if the two of us,
just ran off somewhere and hid?

What if all the crap that we've been through
was a just a storm we were meant to weather?
What if the two of us were always meant,
to spend our last few years together?

What if everything in our lives
was part of a master plan?
What if I was always meant
to eventually become your man?

What if our lives are right on track
for where we're supposed to be?
What if you were always supposed to spend
your *autumn* years with me?

What if everything that's happened,
happened for a reason?
What if one day you decided living with me
is the thing you found most pleasing?

What if everything so far in life,
was only the beginning?
What if we spent our lives together
and no one called it sinning?

What if you were my *valentine*
and I your *Easter bunny*.
What if we spent the rest of our lives
calling each other *Honey*.

I don't have the answers,
But the questions I like to ponder.
When I've nothing else to do,
sometimes I like to sit and wonder.

MY NEW EMAIL FRIEND

She'd been in my thoughts for quite some time.
I'd even dreamt, of her lips on mine.
It could not be, or so it seemed,
but her reality exceeded what I had dreamed.

I was surprised at how my comfort grew
and how my life felt so renewed.
A look or smile can mean so much,
sometimes even, a gentle touch.

She seemed to feel the same as me.
Who'd have thought that could ever be?
That I could learn to love again,
or that she would be my email friend?

Our trip north, was a trial run.
I had only imagined it could be such fun.
But, she's awakened something from deep within,
something I never expected to feel again.

I can't remember a kiss so sweet,
or when my life has felt so complete.
I now look forward instead of back,
I feel my life taking a different track.

I can hardly wait for her next trip *South*,
or to place my lips upon her mouth,
to dance with her, or go out to eat,
to say I love you and then repeat.

MEANT TO BE

Like the wind in the trees,
or the sand and the sea,
you belong with me,
it was simply meant to be.

Like red, white and blue,
or a cow and it's moo,
until you say we're through,
I belong with you.

Like birds of a feather,
Michigan and bad weather,
now and forever,
we belong together.

Like the earth needs the sun,
or a bullet needs a gun,
if I'm ever again to have fun,
you are the one.

Like *Batman* needs *Robin*,
or thread needs a bobbin,
Baby I need you
to keep me from sobbin'.

Like *Tarzan* needs *Jane*,
or a track needs a train,
I think that it's plain,
 you keep me sane.

Like surf goes with turf,
pleasure with mirth,
I'll always need you,
to feel my true worth.

I feel as close to you
as my foot to my shoe,
but it never will do,
unless you feel it too.

Like a really fine wine,
we must take our time,
though come rain or shine,
someday you'll be mine.

MISSING YOU

Seems we've been apart so long
my arms just plain forgot.
Is this how you hold her?
Maybe,,,,,,,,, maybe not.

My arms may want to hold you,
but they're more than willing to share.
They've offered to let my hands
run their fingers through your hair.

My lips just can't remember,
is this the shape we make?
When she gets close to us,
should we give or should we take?

My tongue has been so lonely
it asked me what's the deal?
You should use me for something
besides tasting every meal.

My fingers want to touch you,
just try to cop a feel.
Then they'll ask their neighbors,
is it Memorex, or is she real?

My brain thinks that it's in love
my heart believes it too.
I ask them who they're in love with,
they both claim it's you.

My *Willie* wants to snuggle,
said he'd like to be your pal.
Said, if you'd be his forever
he'd forsake every other gal.

My whole body's bearing up
and it appears that I'll survive.
Just knowing that I'll see you soon
makes me so happy to be alive.

A GIRL LIKE MINE

She'd never *be* with a man
that she didn't choose.
And there's no way he'd ever be cursed
with too many *honey do's*.

When a girl the likes mine
has a guy she really misses,
there's no way he could ever,
give her too many kisses.

He could never too often,
compliment her jugs.
And, there's no way he could ever,
give her too many hugs

He couldn't tell her too often,
she has lots of class.
Nor, could he too often tell her,
she has a really great ass.

She'd never have too much jewelry
and never too many flowers.
Even if they lived
in the fabled *ivory tower*.

She couldn't have too many closets,
and never too many clothes.
Never could she be taken to,
 too many picture shows.

She could never have too much house.
Never too much yard.
Never could he send her,
too many loving cards.

She'll never have too much money
and never too many rings.
There's no way she could ever have
too many of the nicer things.

She could never have too much chocolate,
never too many shoes.
And, no way she could ever hear
too many *I love you's*.

ALWAYS

I was always meant for you.
You were always meant for me.
It was always meant to be that way
and always, it will be.

You're always in my thoughts,
with every breath I take.
You're always in my dreams,
even when I'm wide awake.

When I fall asleep
I always wake to find,
during every waking moment,
you're always on my mind.

When you e-mail me a kiss
it always makes me shiver.
When we talk of making love,
I always hope I can deliver.

You're always in my arms,
even when you're miles away.
That's the way it always is
and always it will stay.

We'll always be together,
even when we are apart.
It's that way because,
you're always in my heart.

WHERE DO WE GO FROM HERE

You're the most important thing to happen,
since the day I lost my wife.
Right now, you're all that matters.
You've given meaning to my life.

I'm not certain where we're headed,
I just know I like the trail.
But, really I'm not certain,
should we raise or lower the sail?

Are we on a collision course?
Is it time to apply the brakes?
Should we just enjoy the ride?
No matter what direction it takes?

Could there ever be another,
who could answer every need?
Should we throw caution to the wind,
just let our hearts take the lead?

You know how much I care for you,
I know that you care for me.
What more must we have,
to live life fancy free?

We've both had reservations,
like rational people would have,
but I think that we could heal them,
let our passion be the salve.

If it's really meant to be,
if we were meant to be together,
there isn't any storm
that this love of ours can't weather.

If it wasn't meant to be,
and under the cover of night,
Old Man Time tries to break us up,
he's in for one hell of a fight.

WOULD YA?

If you were my queen,
and were I really a *king*.
Would you love me as much?
Would I make your heart sing?

If I were the *President*
and you, my *First Lady,*
as part of our family,
would we have a *First Baby*?

If I were a mechanic
and you, a movie star,
would you even look at me,
while I worked on your car?

If I were a long distance runner
and you were my girl.
If I asked you to run away with me,
would you give it a whirl?

If I were a younger man,
not so old and tired,
would you give me a chance?
Would you *rekindle my fire*?

If we spent all our time together,
even through the stress and strife,
could you be happy with me
for the rest of my life.

If you can answer yes,
to these questions I have asked,
we have a much brighter future
than our most recent past.

MY PERFECT MATCH

I had heard of computer dating.
If you haven't, you've been *nappin.'*
But, you could never have convinced me
that this could ever happen.

If you've ever loved and lost
you'll know just what I mean.
All that follows either *is* or *isn't,*
or it's somewhere in between.

Once you've been there,
then through death, have lost it,
you desperately want it back,
but it's hard to find that perfect fit.

For over 20 years
I had involved myself in the search
and yes, I had tried some things
you wouldn't talk about in church.

But, always in the back of my mind
I knew she'd finally show.
When you find that perfect one,
somehow you just seem to know.

For me that day finally arrived
over a dish of *Butter Pecan.*
It was just a little over a year ago,
but I knew my search was done.

We'd been talking through the network,
seems like a little over a month,
but after that first dish of ice cream
I simply knew it all at once.

I already knew her personality,
from everything she'd written.
And, even before we first met,
I knew that I'd been *smitten*.

She'd met all of my criteria
and I'd met most of hers.
We were heading down that road again,
wary of dangerous curves.

But, it seemed real comfortable
from our very first hello.
Can't say I've ever felt that feeling
with others I'd come to know.

To meet that special person
by simply punching some keys?
Seemed like, maybe it could happen,
but probably not for me.

Now, I'm here to tell you friend,
that's just how it came to pass.
I finally met that special one,
she really is first class.

This is my perfect *match,*
we both knew it before we met.
Now for better than a year
life's been perfect as perfect gets.

If they're looking for an endorsement,
or they'd like me to testify,
I'll be the first in line
to suggest you give it a try.

CHAPTER ELEVEN
MY IMAGINATION RUNS WILD

This first poem pretty much explains the entire chapter. All of the poems which came *"mostly from my imagination"* wound up here. There is very little truth in any of them. I often just pick a subject and see where my mind takes me.

ABOUT THIS CHAPTER

Everything in this chapter
is a figment of my imagination.
If there was any truth to it,
this chapter was not it's destination.

Sometimes it comes easy,
other times it's rather tough.
Still, I'm here to tell you,
that I made up all this stuff.

All the other chapters
had some sort of reason,
but mostly I wrote this chapter
just because I found it pleasing.

I just think of things I want to say,
then try to make it rhyme.
Sometimes I have success,
though I'm usually just wasting time.

I spent most of this morning,
re-typing an older poem.
It's different than others I've written,
and it needed a separate home.

So I started a separate file
for poems I consider X-rated.
It's for *ADULTS ONLY*
and it's where that one is definitely slated.

Other poems are about condolences
in a chapter called *SYMPATHETIC WORDS*
and there's a chapter called *LIFE'S LESSONS*
some might say is for the birds.

There are several other chapters
I don't feel the need to explain.
Some are about having fun
others about living through some pain.

Some poems are about remembering,
others about trying to forget,
but if that's been my objective
it hasn't happened yet.

Writing has been great therapy,
especially during times of depression
and whenever I was lonely,
I'd start another writing session.

Sometimes I write about crazy things,
or things that are kinda chancy.
Often it's about my daydreams,
or something else that strikes my fancy.

All sorts of crazy stuff
is destined for this chapter.
Stuff about wild women,
or to bring on a little laughter.

Things I thought might make a song
or that I've heard people sing about.
Things that might make a person cry
or maybe make them pout.

When all is said and done
if it doesn't fit some other place,
you'll probably find it here
if I don't run out of space.

SOMEBODY STOLE FRIDAY

Don't know how it happened,
but time has finally slipped away.
I went to bed Thursday night
and woke up Saturday.

When I went to get my paper,
it was Friday, I would swear.
But, when I opened it up
it said Saturday, right there.

When I went to my pill box,
it happened once again.
There was just an empty space
where my Friday pills had been.

Talk about time *flyin'*
it even disappears.
Days and weeks and months,
somehow turn into years.

Just a short time ago,
I still felt like a kid.
When suddenly all my energy,
ran off somewhere and hid.

Seems like only yesterday
I retired from Peoples Bank.
Still full of piss & vinegar,
now there's nothing in my tank.

I don't know how it happened,
but suddenly I'm old.
It's been over 20 years,
since my life was put on hold.

Now my Friday's missing
and Saturday's going fast.
Then, next thing you know,
another whole year has passed.

A NEW BEGINNING

She was a northern girl,
down for just a short stay.
He lived there,,,,
but, they were both ready to play.

She was younger than him,
but, he'd been with younger.
She had great passion,
and he,,,, a burning hunger.

"What happens in Mexico,
stays in Mexico," says she.
"My name's Jose" he says,
"would you take a ride with me?"

She carried a burden.
He had lived beyond his.
She wasn't ready for him,
not everyone is.

They connected it seemed,
of course, they were both beyond ready.
If it had have been 30 years earlier
he'd have asked her to go steady.

She left him there,
after some passionate kisses,
knowing now what it was,
that his lonely life misses.

He had fantasized about her,
in his house all alone.
He wished she'd come back,
turn his house into a home.

Life still could be fun,
he was now convinced.
He now looks for someone
who'll turn him into her prince.

KEYS TRIP – DAY ONE

I'm in the Florida Keys
with some of my family.
I'm wishing that my dream girl
could have come along with me.

It's 7 o'clock in the morning
as I lie here in my bed.
Thoughts of a sexy blonde
keep running through my head.

As I look out over the ocean
from the balcony of my room,
I keep thinking that my dream girl
better appear real soon.

Someday we'll be together,
we'll lie side by side
and when we do lie down together,
we'll take each other on that *ride.*

Out the door and on our way
to breakfast by the bay.
We'll look for lots of fun things
to do and see today.

This place has such great beauty
of which, I've often read.
I should be drinking in that beauty,
but I dream of her, instead.

We ate dinner at the Lora-lie,
a fantastic seafood platter.
All of us enjoyed the night
and that's what seemed to matter.

We listened to live music,
he played a *Buffett* tune.
The thought occurred that she and I
could be sharing this same moon.

My dream girl should be with me,
but she's in some imaginary land.
This trip would have been for both of us,
if it had been the way I planned.

Of all the things to think about
and all the things to see,
I think about my dream girl
and hope she dreams of me.

KEYS TRIP - DAY TWO

Today we walked the foot path
of an old coral quarry.
It tells about the history
of Florida's early days of glory.

We ate dinner at a seafood place
that looked out across the bay.
And, even with no one beside me,
it was such a lovely day.

We did a little shopping,
then went back to our room.
I stepped out on the balcony
and gazed up at the moon.

It was round and full and beautiful
and it glistened in the waves.
Although she's not here to see it
it's a sight I'll always save.

The night is clear, the stars are out
there's a slight hint of a breeze.
With a glass of brandy in my hand,
I imagine she's with me.

It's Friday night and the full moon
shines down over the ocean.
And, after all the days events
I'm filled with such emotion.

At one o'clock in the morning
the air is very still.
The moon still shines on the water
and I just can't get my fill.

It's a cloudless night and very bright
and it seems so very quiet.
I think about the things we'll do,
if we ever get the chance to try it.

In the morning we'll head home
and I'll think of her some more.
Someday maybe she'll spend time with me
between these two wonderful shores.

FORGETFUL

When I get into the shower,
I try to plan ahead,
I take the phone and my glasses,
but sometimes forget my towel instead.

So, when you finish the job
and are ready to dry yourself,
soaking wet, you cross the room
to get a towel from the shelf.

Seems, I'm getting so forgetful,
it's causing me concern.
Many things, I do by *rote,*
I just do them in their turn.

Well, once you're in the tub
and the water begins to splatter,
the rest just seems to comes natural,
the process doesn't really matter.

The other day, after I'd finished
and had already used the squeegee,
I was reaching for the towel
when a thought occurred to me.

For some reason I couldn't remember,
had I shampooed my hair?
As I stepped out to towel off
I caught myself in a stare.

I stepped in front of the medicine chest,
then I glanced into the mirror.
I had shampooed, but hadn't rinsed
and it was all so perfectly clear.

Every now and then,
seems I have a *brain fart.*
I can't remember if I've finished,
or was I just getting ready to start?

I've always been forgetful,
though it seems to be getting worse.
But, I think that I could deal with it
if I had a pretty blonde nurse.

FOREVER

She wants me to say *forever*
to tell the truth, that's been on my mind.
But, I'm afraid that her *forever*,
might last much longer than mine.

Life *forever* changes,
each and every single day.
Sometimes we go in the same direction.
Sometimes we go our separate way.

Sometimes we get to thinking
that ours is the only way.
If she just doesn't agree,
forever should she stay?

I never want to argue,
I just don't like to fight.
When you see couples doing that,
their *forever* is coming in sight?

I'm not the kind of guy
who has more than one lover at a time.
Still, I'm looking for the perfect one,
meant *forever* to be mine.

I've never believed that love should hurt,
forever causing pain.
That might be the time to call it off,
to "come in out of the rain."

I'd like, *forever* to live my life
with someone that I enjoy.
But, when it's no longer fun,
she should find another toy.

And if the time should ever come,
for our *forever* to end,
she might no longer be my lover,
but *forever* she'll be my friend.

LIFE'S LONELY ROAD

Drivin' down *Old Dixie*,
in this car my buddy loaned,
it's been a long and lonely life,
the last half spent half stoned.

In my mind *she's* right beside me,
heading to a picture show.
She's always by my side
no matter where I go.

Listening to the stereo,
re-living those old times.
George and Merle and Marty
singing those old classic lines.

On Saturday's it's college ball
Sunday it's the professional game.
I really don't enjoy it,
but, every weekend it's the same.

Then it's Monday night football,
Tuesday, back to the mine.
One day after another,
they all fall in line.

Wednesday I meet my buddy
to shoot a game of pool.
He's betting pretty heavy
and I'm taking him to school.

Thursday night it's TV,
Friday night the bar.
It's so close that I can walk it
rather than take my car.

The games start again on Saturday,
friendly wagers declare our pride.
Travelin' down life's lonely road,
with no one to share the ride.

THE DAILY GRIND

I roll out of my bed
and onto my feet.
It's coffee and the sports page,
then rustle up something to eat.

Turn on the stereo
shuffle's the setting.
Hope you like country music,
mostly that's what you'll be getting.

If it's Sunday
I'll be mowing the grass.
If it's any other day,
I'll probably just sit on my ass.

Sometimes in the evening
I'll give *Mom* a call.
If I time it just right
I can also give Karen my all.

When Monday comes around,
the phone starts in about eight.
I always try to answer
I wouldn't dare hesitate.

It could be a customer
wanting us to enter a quote,
but it's more likely a telemarketer
or someone asking for my vote.

Usually in mid afternoon,
I'll simply divorce the phone.
I might slip out for lunch
but, I'll probably go alone.

Most days I'm on the computer
but, I've never done any surfing.
I do proposals for my son,
I like to call it working.

I'll check out my e-mail
to see what I might find.
If it's incoming jokes,
I'll try to respond in kind.

I don't usually shower,
until I'm going somewhere.
If it's a really slow day,
maybe a few games of solitaire.

Somewhere around five,
once or twice a week,
I'll stop for happy hour
with some friends I'll plan to meet.

Most evenings, I'll listen to music
or, I might watch some TV.
Maybe have a glass of wine.
Maybe two or three.

I have some favorite shows
that I just never miss.
It's the wonders of Tivo,
which offer rewards like this.

Monday night is my favorite,
during football season.
It's a chance to get out of the house,
using football as the reason.

The rest of the year
I don't favor one night over the other.
But, I'm sure it would be different
if I simply had a lover.

After Monday, the rest of the week
pretty much follows in line.
I'd make plans to do other things,
if, I could only find the time.

Most evenings, if I'm bored,
I might take a little walk.
Friday's a guy sings at the pub
so, I won't even have to talk.

When Saturday finally rolls around
my neighbor's will ask me to golf.
Lately I've said yes a lot,
but my game's been really off.

I used to really enjoy playing.
It was one of my favorite perks.
But, now I'm just so lousy
it seems too much like work.

He generally beats me.
She usually does too.
I don't like getting beat,
but at least, it's something to do.

Then comes another Sunday,
and it all starts over again.
I should get out of this rut
but I'm just not sure that I can.

CHAPTER TWELVE
JUST FOR GIGGLES

This chapter, similar to chapter 11 is primarily from my imagination, however as the title suggests, it's a little more fun. There may be a little more truth herein, but I'm looking at it from the most humorous side.

MY REMEMBERER IS BROKE

I've forgotten what I can't remember,
or can't remember what I forgot.
This remembering thing is a problem,
cause I think it happens quite a lot.

The things I can't remember
seem to slip right out of my mind.
I can't remember why it happens,
but it seems to happen all the time.

I leave myself reminder notes,
then can't remember where I left them,
and since I've forgotten where they are,
It's more than likely to happen again.

When I do find one of my notes,
can't remember what it's about.
Likely, if they were more complete,
they'd carry a lot more clout.

I seldom remember what I've forgotten,
though I'll remember that I forgot.
Sometimes I'll be reminded,
but after the fact, likely as not.

But, now on my computer
there's a calendar in my software
and if I remember to remind myself,
I can find the answer there.

So now, my daily chore
to keep my mind fancy free,
remember to turn on my computer
and send a reminder note to me.

THE SECOND WEEK OF DEER CAMP

The second week of deer camp
was a song we used to hear.
Seemed like it was written about
the guys in our camp each year.

During that second week
we rarely spotted any deer.
Though, you could bet your 30/30
we'd drink a lot of beer.

It's been nearly 20 years
since I made that annual trek
and my only chance for a deer
was if some one stacked the deck.

But, I learned to drink some beer
and the way the cards are dealt.
We played on an old oak table
and there wasn't any felt.

The Indians were yet to take over
the gambling in the state.
The cards were dealt even before
we'd washed the last dirty plate.

We called it playing poker,
but that's not what it really was.
Poker doesn't have wild cards,
or players as wild as us.

One game was called blind football,
fours were wild and matched the pot.
Sixes cost a quarter, but for deuces
another card was all you got.

The game was pretty nasty,
five of a kind would often win.
And, if even with a great hand
no one could go "all in."

The pots were often huge,
fortunes could be made.
Well, maybe not real fortunes,
but it was the nastiest game we played.

We also played a game called 7/27,
real nasty as I recall,
you could bluff and win a lot,
or you could damn near lose it all.

Craddock was our cook,
mostly, the food was good,
but he knew a trick or two
and he'd trick you if he could.

If you think there are any restaurants
where you can't trust the cook,
the second week of deer camp
will make you take a second look.

You might eat day old pancakes
even the birds wouldn't touch.
And, if you think that those were raisons
you 're not used to *thinking* very much.

But in general, I'd have to say
the food was pretty damn good.
You'd think a guy might lose some weight,
but I swear I never could.

Course, I seldom left the cabin
and I usually drank a lot
and going out to the ol *two holer*
was about all the exercise I ever got.

We heated with an old wood stove
with a milk can sitting on the top.
That's how we got hot water,
but that's not all we got.

When you first arrive at camp,
the milk can needs to be filled
and if your boots sit under the spickett
the laughter will never be stilled.

Dwight was always one of the first
with some nasty little dig,
but when it happens to him
he doesn't handle it very big.

Course, wet boots first day of camp
could get you a little pissed,
but they'd have been a lot wetter
if most of it hadn't missed.

One year Hanks got lost
and we all worried a lot.
Well, that is except for the guys
who put a claim in for his cot.

Seems it was after midnight
when he finally made it back.
We should have had his stuff packed
and a new sleeping bag on his rack.

The guys who brought him in
said he was only 15 miles away.
He should have covered more ground
after all, he'd been gone all day.

He was a real rascal,
quick with a nasty trick,
cigarette loads & firecrackers
were but a small part of his shtick.

One year he flew his *Go Blue* shirt
after a victory won.
Thought he'd rub it in a bit
and have a little fun

Then Trafford said, "They'll shoot it,"
so he quickly changed the plan.
Stuffed it full of *Green and White*,
then put it up again.

Nice sweaters don't belong
as Woody that week learned.
Full of holes or not
somehow it got returned.

Once a case of cheap wine
was left sitting outside the door.
It froze up and busted,
then melted all over the floor.

I always knew the stuff was cheap
and didn't contain much booze,
but it's still better in the stomach
than it is all over your shoes.

Tricks are often funny,
some are nasty too,
but heading for your blind at 3 AM
isn't something most would do.

Yet that's exactly what happened
to Tom and Bob one year.
They'd hardly left the cabin,
when we all got up to cheer.

Someone had changed their watches.
Someone else, the alarm clock.
The fact that they actually fell for it
had us all completely in shock.

When the sun didn't come up by eight
they both began to wonder.
When if finally came up at noon
they figured out they'd made a blunder.

Tom was so easy going
and he could really take a joke.
Bob? Maybe not so much,
but to get even, he'd go for broke.

We'd tend to get a little *gamey*
cause the camp didn't have a shower.
But when the boys went into town
they smelled pretty as a flower.

Amazing what you can cover
with Right Guard and after shave.
Like the old saying goes
"Where there's a will there's a way."

Once we went to a health club
to use their showers and steam room.
Later we came out,
feeling really clean and groomed.

Another time a bunch of us rented a motel
just to use their head.
Surely they wondered about the extra towels,
but nothing was ever said.

During the second week of deer camp
hunting isn't our main mission.
Just like when we go after smelt or Coho
it isn't all about the fishin'.

Sometimes boys just need to be boys.
It's part of our DNA
and the only way we can do it
is to occasionally get away.

I spent many years on the job
but that week in late November?
Well, it contains 75% of the memories
I'm still able to remember.

MAYBE GOLF'S NOT MY GAME

For nearly an hour,
I putted and chipped.
Now it's obvious to me,
my game really has slipped.

I used to have fun
but now it's a bore.
I'm scoring five's & six's
where I used to score four.

Now, I'm pulling most of my irons
and slicing all of my drives.
On most of the par threes,
I'm more likely to score fives.

When it comes to equivalence fours
I'm taking six's & seven's.
Once, I hit two out of bounds
and wound up with an eleven.

I'm slicing so badly
it's affecting my putts.
I've tried so many stances
the guys all think I'm nuts.

I haven't taken any lessons,
but I've read all the books.
I can't cure my slice,
cause sometimes it hooks.

This game, if you let it,
will drive you half crazy.
I need lots more practice,
but I'm just too damn lazy.

I've started taking a *Mulligan*
off the first tee.
And, after only one beer
I already have to pee.

My eyesight's gone bad,
so I bought new glasses.
Thought of giving the game up,
but the feeling soon passes.

From out in the fairway,
those rare times that I'm there,
I can't see the flag,
but my opponents don't care.

We often play for skins
with bets on the side.
They should offer me strokes,
but it would injure my pride.

We'll play *bingo bangle bongo*
in a foursome sometimes.
It's for quarters or dollars,
when it used to be for dimes.

It's a dollar for closest
on all the Par three's.
It's automatic
so, I drop to my knees.

Praying won't help
with a game such as mine,
but there are only 4 Par three's,
I'm so lucky there aren't nine.

Sometimes we'll scramble,
if we have enough players
and the team stuck with me
always says lots of prayers.

One of the reasons
I thought of giving up the game,
is I'm running out of excuses
and they're all sounding so lame.

I've tried new equipment
and bought the new longer ball,
but the further I hit it,
the grass gets more tall.

I've tried a glove on each hand
and tried going without.
The worse I miss-hit it,
the more that I pout.

I've tried the new rescue clubs
and dozens of new putters,
but the harder I try
the more I seem to mutter.

I score mostly *Bogie's*
cause I can't chip worth a damn.
And, after most of my putts
I have to putt it again.

I might pitch it close
then miss the damn putt.
I've been this way all year,
so, I'm not just in a rut.

When your short game goes,
the way that mine has gone,
you should head for the beach
and start wearing a thong.

But, I'm just not quite ready
to give this all up.
So, I open another beer
and pour it into my cup.

I might have the yips,
though I'm not really sure,
but if you don't know what's wrong
you just can't find the cure.

Last time I went out,
I had a bad case of the shanks.
They wanted to play nine more,
but I told them, no thanks.

Now, I'm so damn worried
it might mess up my game,
that I dreamed last night
I'd made the shanker's hall of fame.

Mosquitoes and fire ants,
bruises and bumps.
Water holes and sand traps,
I've taken my lumps.

But a missed two footer,
or an obvious shank,
makes a man start to wonder
about what's left in his tank.

So, I open another beer,
take out another ball,
practice my stance,
then give it my all.

I don't think about "Birdies"
but with an occasional Par,
I keep thinking my game
can't be off all that far.

Finally the nineteenth hole
is coming in sight.
Three of four more beers
might be just about right.

If you're a senior citizen,
they discount your greens fee.
It's the cheapest part of the day,
when you play bad as me.

The game is expensive
with equipment and all,
but it's settling my bets
where I really take the fall.

But, as we gather at the bar,
and I settle my bets,
I think to myself
this is as good as it gets.

Birdies and Par's
most likely are all in my past,
but you can bet I'll keep swinging
hoping this day won't be my last.

SOME DAYS

Some days you're the slingshot,
other days the stone.
There are days you just get tired
of living all alone.

Some days you're the swatter,
other days the fly.
Either you're ecstatic,
or just barely getting by.

Some days you're the fuel,
other days the flame.
You know that you've been lonely
and you know just whom to blame.

Some days you're the wind,
other days the sail.
Sometimes you'd like someone
to help when you need to bale.

Some days it's a slap,
other days a hug.
You want someone to care for,
but you don't like feeling bugged.

Some days you're the fire hydrant,
other days the dog.
Lately it just seems like
you've been living in a fog.

Some days you're the trainer,
other days the whip.
Some days you're afraid
you might be losing your grip.

Some days you're the tiger,
or you've got it by the tail.
You're either making progress,
or getting set to fail.

Some days you're the grill,
other days the meat.
Some times all of us
must take a little heat.

Some days you're the oyster,
other days the pearl.
Sometimes all you think about
is your desire for that girl.

Some days you're the eraser,
other days the chalk.
Sometimes all you want
is to sit with her and *talk*.

Some days you're the mower,
other days, the grass.
You know that she's special,
but she might be out of your class.

Some days you're the frying pan,
other days, the fire.
Sometimes you need to take a chance
and seek out your desires.

Some days you're the ax,
other days the tree.
Eventually you must make a choice,
cause your freedom isn't really free.

Some days you're the early bird,
other days the worm.
You're convinced she cares for you,
a fact that she's confirmed.

241

Some days you're the stopper,
other days the jug.
You know there are times,
when both of you need a little hug.

Some days you're the hammer,
other days the nail.
Sometimes it depends upon
if she sent you any mail.

Some days you're the matador,
other days the bull.
She's very much in your heart
and it's feeling nearly full.

Some days it's foul,
other days it's fair.
Though, the two of you are close,
you're still not quite a pair.

Some days you're the pooch,
other days the flea.
For now it's she and I,
but maybe someday we'll be we.

Some days you're the rainbow,
other days the rain.
You've lived separate lives
and each has known some pain.

Some days you're the worm,
other days the hook.
Sometimes our relationships
don't go by the book.

Some days are much better,
some, considerably worse.
But today, she's in your thoughts
and this day is not the first.

Some days you're the windshield,
other days the bug.
You know if she were here just now,
you'd do more than kiss & hug.

Some days you're the brass monkey,
other days just the balls.
You really want to share her life,
but are you ready to give your all?

Some days you're the lightning,
other days the thunder.
You'd like to light up her life,
but you worry about making a blunder.

Some days you're the butcher,
other days you're his knife.
You know you want to be with her,
but you're not ready for a wife.

Some days you're the target,
other days the arrow.
You think she really cares for you,
but are you thinking kind of narrow?

Some days you're the gun,
other days, the hammer.
Some days what you want to do
is strip her down and slam her.

Some days you're the horse,
other days the horse's a...
She'll likely know the difference,
if you show a little class.

Some days you're the football,
other days the kicker.
You'd like to share this poem with her,
but you're afraid she'd only snicker.

Some days you're the bat,
other days the ball.
If you ever decide to share it
you'll be the one to make that call.

CHAPTER THIRTEEN
PURSUIT REWARDED

I'm now in my mid sixty's, hoping to make the best of the time that I have left. I've met a wonderful lady and I now look forward to every new day. That hasn't always been the case, but I consider myself to be a lucky man. As this first poem says, *I've had a good life*. With the time that I have left, I'm expecting to have a fantastic finish. I may be *nearing the end,* but I still have a lot left in my tank. My life now definitely has new meaning and I firmly believe that my *pursuit* is being *rewarded.*

I expect I will continue to write, because it has become an eternal passion, however I don't expect to devote the time to it that I have in the past. It is unlikely that my writing will ever be read by more than a few close friends and relatives. However, when I began to write I never expected to get to the point that I would share it even with that small audience.

My original choice for a title to this book was *Is There Life After Death?* which we later changed to: *A Pursuit Of Life After Death* and eventually shortened to *A Pursuit Of Life*. Without any consideration for your beliefs, or lack of belief in Heaven and Hell, please trust me, there most definitely is joy in *a pursuit of life after death.*

I'VE HAD A GOOD LIFE

Mostly, it's been a pretty good life
and I've lived most all my dreams.
I've also lived some nightmares,
at least that's the way it seems.

I didn't plan on being single
for all these twenty years,
but no one gets through life
without some occasional tears.

She didn't want to leave me,
nor did I want for her to leave.
And, as the end was near
I tried so very hard to believe.

It still troubles me some,
was I the one to blame?
If I'd have prayed a little harder,
would it have still come out the same?

When we went to that Faith Healer,
if I'd been more convinced,
when he laid hands upon her
would her chances have been enhanced?

I've never had a lot of goals
and none were set too high.
I've never wanted for much,
just wanted to somehow get by.

And those few goals I set,
well I think I attained them all.
There could be one or two I missed,
but none that I recall.

Pretty much, I take life as it comes,
I've never made a lot of plans.
I never planned to be a banker,
never planned on owning land.

Never thought about having a family
or such a wonderful wife.
I've always taken one day at a time
just working my way through life.

I've had a few regrets,
but probably no more than most.
Probably the biggest one I have,
she missed out on the Treasure Coast.

Now that I'm in my sixty's
and the end's just over the horizon,
I've started thinking about my mortality,
guess that's not really so surprising.

There's a lady in my dreams
and somewhere she dreams of me.
Some day when we meet
we'll be as happy as can be.

But, it's not all that easy,
awaiting that special day.
I'm afraid we'll run out of time,
still trying to find our way.

Oh, I know she'll be worth the wait
and we'll steal moments here and there,
but I want to be with her now,
we've so much yet to share.

I think about her often,
but for now, I bide my time.
And, I wile away my days
putting thoughts of her in rhyme.

I AIN'T DONE PAYING YET

Well, *I've been down that road*
and I've been *up the creek.*
I'm not *over the hill,*
but I'm getting close to the peak.

If you get what you pay for
and you pay for what you get,
oh Lord, I've been wondering
ain't I done paying yet.

I've been used, abused,
beaten and bruised
and a couple a times,
I've been falsely accused.

I've been called crazy and wild,
a fool and a clown.
For a time I was cheered
and once nearly drowned.

I've been rode hard and I've rode hard,
been driven and tried.
Been balled out and *called out,*
been beaten and I've cried.

I've been yelled at and spit on,
been made a fool
and more than once,
I've been *taken to school.*

I've been looked up to and down on
respected and feared.
Been cheated and lied to,
been accused and was cleared.

I've bombed and been busted,
broken and hog tied
and a time or two
it's likely I've lied.

Been down in the oil fields,
dug coal in the mines,
spent time as a lumberjack
way out in the pines.

I've been to the end of my rope
and seen the end of the line.
I know rocks aren't gold,
but seems that's all my pan ever mines.

I've been stepped on and kicked round,
shit on and shot.
If you consider the possibilities,
I'm lucky that's all I got.

I've *climbed the walls*
and I've *had my back up agin' it*.
And, if money was water,
seen times I couldn't spit.

I've seen mountains and valleys,
deserts and sand.
When it comes right down to it,
I've seen most of this land.

Been locked up and *locked out*,
but recently I've found,
there's an end to this road
that I've been headed down.

Now I've nothing to do,
my remaining life to do it
and if my life has been a job,
it's the first one I didn't quit.

I've been mistreated and misguided
and while traveling around,
been cursed and was *Born Again*
ya might say lost and found.

Yeah, I've been *down that road*,
I've also been *up the creek*,
I'm not over the hill,
but I'm convinced I'll make the peak.

I don't always get what I pay for,
but I always pay for what I get
and yes I'm still wandering,
so I ain't done paying yet.

I'M AT PEACE WITH WHO I AM

I've nothing to do
and my lifetime to do it,
so I have no reason to <u>worry.</u>
I've nowhere to go
and the rest of my life to get there,
so I've no reason to <u>hurry.</u>

I've time on my hands,
without much time left,
but I'm not <u>apprehensive.</u>
I've money to spend,
but nothing to buy,
so it doesn't matter if it's <u>expensive.</u>

I'm a tired, old
and lonely man,
without a lot left to <u>give.</u>
I've nothing to do,
no urgency to do it
and no one to do it <u>with.</u>

The one I loved
is beyond my reach
and I don't seem to ever get <u>better.</u>
But, I guess
I should consider myself lucky
for the time we spent <u>together.</u>

I've been to the top
of the mountain.
I've seen the depths of the <u>valley.</u>
When all is said and done
I've been fortunate, I guess,
'cause I've never slept in an <u>alley.</u>

I've got family,
(two wonderful sons)
and if I still need a reason to <u>live,</u>
my boys, their *wives*
and their beautiful daughters,
can benefit from the little I've left to <u>give</u>.

Probably,
I could have done more with my life,
but I'm just a simple <u>man.</u>
And,
as the end of my journey nears,
I'm at peace with who I <u>am.</u>

MY NEW TOMORROW

I'm getting long in tooth, but
I've realized most all my plans.
It hasn't always been a happy life,
but I've been given another chance.

One day when I awoke,
I found myself looking back.
I'd always been forward thinking,
but somehow I'd gotten a bit off track.

First you're turning sixteen,
then you graduate.
Soon you're married with kids
coming through your front gate.

You've already been to college,
already bought your second home.
The kids are grown and gone,
then you find yourself alone.

You wander for a while,
trying to find your way.
Several wrong paths taken,
lead you to this day.

You've a bunch of yesterdays
with things still left undone.
But, very few tomorrows
to enjoy the rising of the sun.

There's a lady in your life and
you're now long past the *sorrow*.
It's been a long and winding road,
but she's now your *new tomorrow*..

MOVING ON

They said that you're in Heaven
and that I should feel relieved.
I'm yet to be convinced,
but I really tried to believe.

I was glad you no longer suffered
you fought an admirable fight.
They said I'd see you again.
If there's a Heaven, some day I might.

I struggle with their message,
but not the way I've lived my life.
I've tried to honor your memory,
you were an extraordinary wife.

Now it's over twenty years
since we said our last goodbye.
Can't say I've gotten over you,
but I'm finally ready to try.

It's time that I moved on,
too long I've sought your sequel.
I'll be forever happy now,
I believe I've finally met your equal.

LIST OF POEMS

4

40 YEARS TOGETHER – Bill & Carol, 154

5

50 YEARS TOGETHER – Tom & Jean, 156
50th ANNIVERSARY - FOR UNCLE GLEN, 161
50th ANNIVERSARY - FOR AUNT JANE, 159

A

A CHRISTMAS POEM FOR DONNA, 184
A DREAM COME TRUE, 194
A GIRL LIKE MINE, 204
A LOST GEM, 171
A MOTHER'S DAY POEM – FOR MOM, 98
A NEW BEGINNING, 215
A SINGLE MAN I AM, 186
A TRIP TO THE RIVER, 59
ABOUT THIS CHAPTER, 212
ACKNOWLEDGEMENTS, viii
ALL ABOUT ME, 20
ALWAYS, 206
AUNT JANE NINETY?, 163

B

BAD DAYS (For Karen), 77

C

CELEBRATION, 136
CHAPTER 10, 177
CHAPTER 9, 164
CHAPTER EIGHT, 128
CHAPTER ELEVEN, 211
CHAPTER FIVE, 70
CHAPTER FOUR, 55
CHAPTER ONE, 1

CHAPTER SEVEN, 115
CHAPTER SIX, 90
CHAPTER THIRTEEN, 245
CHAPTER THREE, 43
CHAPTER TWELVE, 227
CHAPTER TWO, 23
CHRISTMAS - MOM, 2001, 92
CHRISTMAS 1998, 129
CHRISTMAS AT KEVIN'S, 130
CHRISTY'S CHRISTMAS, 1998, 131
CHRISTY'S GRADUATION, 5ᵗʰ grade 2005, 132

D

DADDY'S WORDS, 73
DID SHE KNOW?, 36
DID WE MAKE YOUR MOMMA PROUD, 37
DREAM OR A NIGHTMARE?, 195

F

FAMILY, 12
FOR LORA, 118
FOR MOTHER'S DAY, 95
FOREVER, 222
FORGETFUL, 220

G

GLEN & JANE - 50 YEARS TOGETHER, 157
GOOD BYE BILLY, 116
GOOD BYE FRIEND, 117
GRANDPA WAYNE, 126

H

HAPPY BIRTHDAY - KAREN, 137
HAPPY BIRTHDAY KYLIE, August 4, 2006, 142
HAPPY BIRTHDAY MARILYN, 150
HAPPY BIRTHDAY MOM - 2005, 104
HAPPY BIRTHDAY MOM 2006, 105
HAPPY BIRTHDAY SIS, 138

I

I AIN'T DONE PAYING YET, 248
I CAN HEAR HER MUSIC, 192
I DON'T BELIEVE, 34

I WANT TO SHARE WITH YOU, 188
I'M AT PEACE WITH WHO I AM, 251
I'VE HAD A GOOD LIFE, 246
I'VE MET A WONDERFUL NEW FRIEND, 42
IF IT WEREN'T FOR BOOZE, 79
INTRODUCTION, ix
IT'S NOT MY JOB, 88

J

JUST 'CAUSE THE CAUSE IS JUST, 86

K

KEYS TRIP – DAY ONE, 216
KEYS TRIP - DAY TWO, 218
KYLIE IN THE KEYS, 143
KYLIE, One year old, 140

L

LIFE'S LONELY ROAD, 223

M

MAYBE GOLF'S NOT MY GAME, 235
MEANT TO BE, 201
MICHIGAN TRIP - Mom's birthday, 99
MISSING YOU, 203
MOM'S 25th ANNIVERSARY June 8, 1998, 112
MOM'S CHRISTMAS POEM - 2005, 91
MOM'S SPECIAL DAY, 97
MOM'S TEETH, 110
MOMS BIRTHDAY 2009, 107
MOVING ON, 254
MY BROTHER, 62
MY DAUGHTER-IN-LAW, SHELLY, 148
MY DREAM GIRL, 196
MY FRIEND LORA, 119
MY GIRL, 24
MY GRANDDAUGHTER RACHEL, 147
MY LIFE - THE MIDDLE YEARS, 6
MY LIFE - TODAY, 10
MY LIFE - TROUBLING YEARS, 9
MY LIFE- THE BEGINNING, 2
MY MATCH, 178
MY MICHIGAN VACATION, 66
MY NEW EMAIL FRIEND, 200

MY NEW FRIEND, 183
MY NEW TOMORROW, 253
MY PERFECT MATCH, 209
MY REMEMBERER IS BROKE, 228

N

NO ONE, 46
NO LONGER ALONE, 198

O

ONE BAD TURN AFTER ANOTHER, 175

P

PATRIOTIC POETRY, 84
PRECIOUS MOMENTS, 52
PRELUDE, vi

Q

QUESTIONS, 181

R

RACHEL IN THE KEYS, 145
RACHEL'S BIRTHDAY, 146
RAISING KIDS, 71
REMEMBERING CHRISTINE, 27
REMINISCENCES, 173
RETURNING HOME, 50

S

SHE, 45
SHE'LL NEVER KNOW, 166
SHE'S ALWAYS STANDING THERE, 32
SOME DAYS, 240
SOMEBODY STOLE FRIDAY, 214
STARTING OVER, 44
STILL MOURNING?, 40

T

TALKING TO CHRISTINE, 29
THANKS VERN & SHIRLEY, 64
THANKSGIVING - 2005, 114

THE DAILY GRIND, 224
THE OLD DAYS, 15
THE REASONS MY BUDDY DRINKS, 81
THE SECOND WEEK OF DEER CAMP, 229
THEN CAME HALLOWEEN, 169
THINKING OF CHRISTINE, 26
TIME TO MOVE ON, 49
TO CAROLYN, 122
TO MY MOM, 94
TOO YOUNG FOR BINGO, 190
TROUBLED WATERS FOR MOM, 124
TURNING THIRTEEN - CHRISTY, 133

U

UNINVITED LOVE, 51

W

WAYNE'S 25th ANNIVERSARY (6/8/98), 152
WHAT IF ?, 199
WHEN THE LOVIN' JUST UP & ENDS, 168
WHERE DO WE GO FROM HERE, 207
WOULD YA?, 208

Y

YEARNING FOR MICHIGAN, 56
YOU CAN'T GO BACK, 165
YOU'RE THE REASON I GO ON, 54
YOU'RE STILL NEEDED, 75

LaVergne, TN USA
30 June 2010
187897LV00009B/96/P